Sleep Thinking

Books by Eric Maisel

NONFICTION

A Life in the Arts
Artists Speak
Fearless Creating
Fearless Presenting
Affirmations for Artists
Deep Writing
Living the Writer's Life
The Creativity Book
20 Communication Tips for Families
20 Communication Tips at Work

FICTION

The Black Narc
The Kingston Papers
Dismay
The Blackbirds of Mulhouse
The Fretful Dancer

The Revolutionary Program that
Helps You Solve Problems, Reduce Stress,
and Increase Creativity While You Sleep

Sleep Thinking

Eric Maisel, Ph.D.
with Natalya Maisel

Adams Media Corporation
Holbrook, Massachusetts

10-01   #45744767

Published by
Adams Media Corporation
260 Center Street, Holbrook, MA 02343
www.adamsmedia.com

ISBN: 1-58062-445-6

Printed in Canada.

J I H G F E D C B

Library of Congress Cataloging-in-Publication Data
available from the publisher.

This publication is designed to provide accurate and authoritative information with regard to the subject matter covered. It is sold with the understanding that the publisher is not engaged in rendering legal, accounting, or other professional advice. If legal advice or other expert assistance is required, the services of a competent professional person should be sought.
 — From a *Declaration of Principles* jointly adopted by a Committee of the American Bar Association and a Committee of Publishers and Associations

This book is available at quantity discounts for bulk purchases. For information, call 1-800-872-5627.

Sleep Thinking and the Sleep Thinking Program are trademarks of Eric Maisel, Ph. D.

for Ann

Contents

Introduction

I started thinking about the ideas in this book more than 30 years ago, when I began writing my first novel. Even back then, I was curious about the workings of the brain during the nighttime. While other people seemed interested in and even obsessed by dreams, I was more taken with the idea of the brain as a nighttime problem-solving organ that never went off line and that needed clear direction if it was going to work effectively during sleep.

I knew from personal experience and from the reports of famous scientists, inventors, and artists that the brain worked—and worked beautifully—while we slept. But at that time, I had no coherent picture of how it could be enlisted to solve problems during the night. I continued writing fiction, trained as a psychotherapist, and became a creativity consultant and college teacher, during which time my interest in the powers of the brain at night intensified.

For the past 15 years, I've worked with creative and performing artists, talking with them about creativity as well as their mental health problems. Out of these experiences have come books on the creative life, including *The Creativity Book, Fearless Creating, Deep Writing,* and *A Life in the Arts.* In addition, for the last 12 years I've helped adult students in their 30s, 40s, and 50s engage in personal and professional assessment as part of their return to college.

As I counseled, taught, interacted with, and learned from all these people, I was continually struck by how much went on in their lives while they were asleep. I listened closely to what they had to say and began to see how they solved problems, worked on creative projects, came up with insights, reduced their stress, and even changed their lives as they slept. I asked a lot of questions. The more I learned, the more comfortable I became with suggesting to new clients that they use sleep as a time to problem solve. In this way, I began to see how sleep thinking could be made into a systematic program.

I enlisted my daughter, Natalya, to help me research the sleep literature. Together we learned about the peculiarities and special function of non-REM (NREM) sleep, listened to the stories of problem solving and creating recounted by sleep subjects, and acquainted ourselves with the standard and more obscure experimental results. I also asked friends and colleagues about their sleep thinking experiences. Because the subject fascinated them, they began to ask *their* friends and colleagues, who in turn communicated their experiences to me.

So this book grew. Some of the stories in this book are direct and unadorned, some are altered to maintain confidentiality, and some are composites put together from the experiences of various people to illustrate the points I want to make. I hope that you'll find the sleep thinking program outlined here both interesting and useful. I firmly believe that if you allow it, sleep thinking can change your life. ((•))

CHAPTER 1

Understanding Sleep Thinking

My goal in this book is to teach you how to use sleep thinking to solve your problems, reduce your stress, upgrade your personality, and increase your creativity. After a bit of an introduction, I'll ask you to begin your own sleep thinking program, which will involve a little self-inquiry, a new bedtime routine, a new morning routine, and a few other changes and additions to your current lifestyle. I hope you'll give this program a try. If you do, your experience will be remarkable.

What exactly is sleep thinking? To put it simply, it is your brain continuing, while your sleep, to work on the issues and problems that matter to you. Your brain performs many functions while you sleep, and productive thinking can be one of them. But in order for your brain to work in an optimal way, it has certain needs; for example, it needs to know what it's being asked to do. You can meet these needs in a simple, straightforward way. Read on.

Sleep thinking is one of the most important basic human skills. Yet most of us have heard little or nothing about it. Perhaps you've heard about a scientist who woke up with the solution to a problem or a writer who woke up with an idea for a book, but that's it. As powerful and profound as sleep thinking is, it has eluded our scrutiny because our attention has been focused solely on dreams. Because dreams are so fascinating and even magical, they have seduced us and lured us away from investigating the powers of the brain during the rest of the sleep cycle.

Dreams are such an exciting phenomenon that they've dominated the brain research and psychotherapeutic landscapes. New books on dream interpretation come out all the time, and experiments on REM sleep (during which dreaming occurs) continue. All the attention paid to dreaming, beginning more than a century ago with Freud's work on the meaning of dreams, has caused us to miss the other extraordinary thing that the brain can do while we sleep.

That other extraordinary thing that your brain can do while you sleep is THINK. It does this primarily during NREM (nonrapid eye movement) sleep. There are two types of sleep: REM sleep, during which most dreaming occurs, and NREM sleep, during which slower wave, higher frequency brain activity occurs. NREM sleep is further divided into four stages. The time between stage 1 of NREM sleep to the first REM sleep is called the first sleep cycle. There are usually about four or five such cycles a night, each lasting about 90 minutes. It is during the NREM portions of the sleep cycle, and especially during stages 2, 3, and 4, when sleeping is deepest that thinking and problem solving occurs.

For many years, people believed that no mental activity occurred during NREM sleep. But during the past few decades, this notion has been proven false. Scientists have discovered that a large amount of high-level activity, including thinking and problem solving, occurs during these stages of sleep. David Foulkes, a sleep researcher, made some important discoveries about NREM sleep and demonstrated that people awakened during NREM sleep often reported that they were thinking. For example, when one subject was awakened, he described how he was trying to answer a question that had been posed in a class he'd been teaching earlier that day. His brain was taking NREM sleep as an opportunity to problem solve and find the right answer. This is typical of NREM sleep; we use it to solve problems of all sorts.

We've all experienced sleep thinking at least occasionally. One of my psychotherapy clients, who was troubled by the way her VCR was acting up, went to bed thinking about what might be wrong with it. When she awoke, she went right to the VCR and fixed it. The solution did not come to her in a dream; it just "came to her," which is how NREM thinking works. We do not experience it as dreaming; we often do not experience it at all. In fact, with this type of thinking, we are entirely unaware that our brain is working on a problem, making connections, and looking for solutions, until the answer "comes out of thin air." We might wake up in the middle of the night with the answer, the answer may be waiting for us when we wake up in the morning, or it might come to us during the day as the sleep thinking we did during the night makes its way into conscious awareness. But, however the answer arrives, it has that well-known "aha!" quality about it, that is, the quality of revelation.

Examples of our own sleep thinking are usually of the following sort. A therapist colleague had this to say:

When I was in college, I took a chemistry course. We were given ten problems to solve and a week in which to turn them in. I liked chemistry and was good at it, so when the answer to one of the ten problems wasn't immediately apparent, I figured I would come back to it later. In no way was I anxious about this or worried or even thinking *it over during the week. Yet, several nights later I woke up with a solution to the problem, and in fact, it was the correct one.*

Another therapist colleague explained:

I clearly remember solving a problem in my sleep. I was doing my undergraduate work in a math class. I had an equation to solve, but when I went to graph the solution, I got half a circle. The answer in the back of the book showed a full circle. It was late, and I was tired, so I went to bed pondering the problem. I awoke in the middle of the night as the answer came to me. I had forgotten that when you take the square root of any number, you get both the positive and the negative value. Problem solved.

These are typical examples of sleep thinking. What they share in common is that the sleep thinker was aware that a certain problem existed and wanted the problem solved. She engaged the problem and let her brain do the thinking for her while she slept. First there was *awareness* of a problem. Then there was a *desire* to solve it (often we do not want to solve our problems because the solution, say a job change or a divorce, feels like a bigger problem), then there was *engagement* with the problem, and finally there was *surrender* to the brain's natural way of working. Awareness, desire, engagement, and surrender are the four key elements of the sleep thinking program.

The sleep thinking program that you'll learn about in this book is designed to help you solve problems while you sleep. These can be the *most important* problems in your life, not just the occasional calculus or biology problem. Your life may feel off-track; sleep thinking can help you find your way. You may be working very hard at a new career but feel as if you're not progressing the way you'd like. Sleep thinking can help you figure out what's wrong and what to do next. You may be having relationship problems with a parent, child, or mate; sleep thinking can get you past the pain and confusion and lead you to a clearer understanding of the problem and then point you in the direction of a solution. Sleep thinking is also the way to incubate creative projects and solve intellectual problems of all sorts. It is a complete idea generation and idea management program, a problem-solving tool of the first magnitude, a stress reducer, and even a treatment for insomnia. Best of all, it is the way your brain really wants to work, if you will just give it permission.

Abby and Her Roommate

Before I lay out the sleep thinking program, I want to preview how sleep thinking can work for you. You'll see in the following vignette the steps that make up the sleep thinking program, steps that we'll explore in detail shortly.

Abby is 19 years old and finishing her first year in college. For the past year, she's been living in the dorms with Jan, her best friend from high school. Soon Abby will need to make up her mind about living arrangements for next year. Jan has been talking about the two of them getting an apartment near campus, but Abby has reservations about this possibility. She has had a good time with Jan but has discovered that Jan is pretty wild and can be very irresponsible.

Jan never cleans up her part of the room, she's always late with the payment for her part of the phone bill, and she's up all hours of the night bringing people back to the room and partying. At the same time, Abby likes it that Jan is so much fun, and she often likes the partying herself. She just wishes that it wasn't all the time and all through the night. She and Jan have been friends for so long that it is hard to imagine parting ways, but she's not sure that she can take another year of Jan's irresponsibility.

As she struggles with whether or not she wants to continue rooming with Jan, Abby hears about sleep thinking from a friend. She decides to try it out, to see whether she can figure out what she really wants to do with respect to Jan and their rooming together. As she's instructed to do, she makes up a list of the first questions that come into her head:

)) Do I want to keep rooming with Jan?
)) Am I willing to risk our friendship by not rooming with her?
)) Do I want to stay friends with her?
)) Can I handle another year with her?
)) Will she get worse when we have our own apartment?

Looking over her list, Abby knows that the main question at hand is whether or not she wants to room with Jan next year. The answers to the other questions also will contribute to her decision, but she thinks that it is best to get to the main point first. So the first night she goes to bed reciting, "Do I want to room with Jan next year?" She generally doesn't have a problem getting to sleep; she's usually thinking about things she *wants* to think about. But it takes a lot of will power to concentrate on this question.

The next morning, Abby wakes up and remembers a dream she had. In her dream, she sees Jan drinking coffee in a cafe. She writes down this dream, although she can't see how it really relates to the problem at hand. She is surprised, though, that she had a dream about Jan. To her knowledge, this is the first dream she has had with Jan in it. So she thinks that at least it is good that her thoughts and dreams became focused on this subject, although she did not receive an answer. She knows that it would probably be helpful if she could really recite her question more like a meditation, and that becomes her objective the next night.

That night Abby gets home late from studying at the library and is very tired by the time she goes to bed. She takes out her journal and looks over the notes she made about the first night she tried sleep thinking. She writes her question one more time: "Do I want to room with Jan next year?" But by the time she hits her pillow, she is so tired that she recites her question only once and falls asleep immediately. Still, she has another dream about Jan. This time she and Jan are talking with Jan's boyfriend, Kyle. They're all laughing together about something.

Abby can't see how this dream might answer her question. She only sees that she and Jan are having a good time together, but she doesn't know whether that means that she and Jan should stay roommates. Abby has always known that she and Jan have fun together; the problem occurs when Jan goes too far. So Abby doesn't feel as if this has brought up any new thoughts or solved her problem. She writes the dream down and doesn't try to analyze it any further.

On the third night, she sees similar results. She has a dream in which she is in the dorm room that she now shares with Jan. She is hanging up a new poster of a band that Jan likes. Abby records this but, again, doesn't know what to make of it. She does find it interesting, though, that for the past three nights she has had dreams that had to do with the question she was asking. She is surprised by how quickly everything she dreams about has become focused on this question. But she is still having trouble reciting her question in a meditative way.

The fourth night, she goes to bed and decides that she will spend extra time repeating her question. So she says it over and over again. Finally, she falls asleep. The next morning, she can't remember any dreams at all. She finds it odd that on the night she managed to repeat her question several times, she had no dreams she could remember. She takes a few minutes to think about the way that she said her question. She realizes that she said it harshly, as though it were a chore—something that she needed to get done. She can still hear herself saying, almost angrily, "Do I want to room with Jan?" Saying it that way didn't put her into a contemplative state. So she decides that this has to change if she wants to see results; she has to become relaxed and at ease with saying her question.

On the fifth night, Abby doesn't follow through with her plans. She falls asleep before she can recite her question even once. In the morning, she wakes with the slight remembrance of a dream that had to do with Jan, but she can't remember what it was about. She is getting a little upset by her lack of will power and her inability to go to bed early and really prepare herself for sleep thinking.

As this process is going on, things with Jan remain pretty much the same. Jan is still partying a lot, and Abby is more torn about her own feelings. On the sixth day, Jan and Abby have a nice lunch together, and Jan brings up seeing a table in a store that she thinks would look great in their apartment next year. Abby ends up feeling more confused.

On the sixth night, Abby stays up with her friend Carly watching a movie starring Mel Gibson. She goes to bed tired and, against her own wishes, falls right asleep. That night she has a dream about being in a big table store. That's all she remembers about the dream, although she thinks that Mel Gibson might have been the sales clerk. Abby feels that the dream was influenced by the events of her day rather than by anything having to do with her question.

On the seventh night, Abby finds that she's able to say her question a little more gently than usual. She's also able to repeat it quite a few times before falling asleep. In the morning, she recalls the dream she had and writes it down. In the dream, she and Jan were in their room, and Jan was making phone calls. Abby wanted to tell Jan to hang up the phone. She's surprised that yet another dream has focused on her question, but she still doesn't know what to do, although she realizes that her dream brought up her anger toward some of Jan's behavior.

On the eighth night, Abby gets home quite late and falls asleep as soon as she gets into bed. In the morning, she has no recollection of any dreams.

On the ninth night, Abby really tries to make some progress. She turns down an offer to watch another movie and goes to bed a little earlier than normal so that she is not "too tired." When she gets into bed, she says her question particularly gently and several times over before she falls asleep.

That night she has a dream that she feels may be the answer to her question. She wakes up in the morning and writes down her dream. The first thing she writes down is the word *intense*. She seems to know that this dream is important. In this dream, Abby is at a concert with Jan. Jan is screaming and dancing all over the place. Abby is trying to hear the music, but she can't because Jan is behaving so wildly. Jan spills her drink all over Abby and doesn't stop to apologize or help her. Abby leaves Jan in the stands, saying, "I've had enough." Then she moves down closer to where the band is playing. The last thing that Abby remembers about the dream is a song with these lyrics:

"Go back and say something. Go back and say something."

In the morning, Abby feels good about this dream. She feels that it is different from the others. She writes down all that she can remember. Although some of the other dreams seemed more related to the main point (of whether to room together), such as the one in their dorm room, no dream has felt as important as this one. She's purposefully been avoiding analyzing her dreams because she hasn't felt that they were worth analyzing, but she thinks about this dream and sees that two main things are happening: Jan is acting in the way that Abby fears she will always act, and Abby seems not to be able to take it anymore. In addition, the song was telling her to go back and talk to Jan. Abby thinks that the point of the dream may be that she has to tell Jan that she is having real problems with some of her behavior.

The dream has made her more sure of what she must do, though she knows that it will not be easy for her. She needs to figure out what to say to Jan about what she is feeling. So she decides to do some more sleep thinking.

The new question she poses to herself is: How can I talk to Jan about her behavior? This time, to her surprise, Abby gets an answer right away, the very first night, and not in the form of a dream. She wakes up and knows that she must "just do it." This makes sense to her, but she can't make herself talk to Jan that day or the next—or even hint at the fact that something is bothering her.

What she realizes is that the sleep thinking process got her to a place she intuitively understood already, that she did not want to room with Jan in the coming year but that she was going to have a hard time telling Jan the truth, so hard a time that she might just end up rooming with her anyway. Abby doesn't want this to happen, and finally she does approach the matter. To her surprise, Jan has been thinking the same thing. Jan says that a couple of new friends of hers have been discussing getting an apartment together and have invited Jan to join them. Though she has been thinking about saying yes, she didn't want to put Abby in a bind or hurt her feelings.

By the end of their chat it's clear to Abby that this phase of her life is ending, that she won't be seeing Jan very much in the future, and that now she'll have to think about what she wants to do next. She also realizes that sleep thinking allowed her to arrive at the truth of the matter, that she needed to talk with Jan or else risk a difficult, distracting sophomore year. Her problems are not solved entirely, because now she'll have to find a new roommate, one who no doubt will present her with new problems and challenges. But she's pleased that she thought about her problem, rather than ignoring it.

$Q.$ *Is sleep thinking really any different from plain old garden variety thinking?*

It is. The difference is both in the quantity and the quality of the brain work involved. During the day, we're rarely able to devote all or even much of our mental resources to a given problem or idea. The phone interrupts us. A task interrupts us. We get hungry. We get mentally tired. Some other thought intrudes and sends us off in another direction. The phone rings again. E-mail piles up. It's time for lunch. In other words, our days are fractured and busy, and other wants and needs intrude.

During the night, our brain can just think. To use a technical phrase, larger neuronal gestalts get to form: that is, more neurons are freed from their customary duties and can band together, making for an enormous army that can attack any question. If you're interested in how neuronal gestalts work, check out Susan Greenfield's *Journey to the Centers of the Mind*. It's a real eye-opener. Your brain is much more fluid and plastic than you might think, and it can operate narrowly or more expansively, depending on circumstances. Nighttime provides the right set of circumstances.

There are probably other, currently unknown differences between awake thinking and sleep thinking as well. It's possible that the thing we call the unconscious is best accessed by sleep thinking. Who can say? When we sleep, we may also have access to so many memories, so much uncensored material, and so many images and feelings that we may be talking about a way of thinking that is quantitatively and qualitatively different from awake thinking. Sleep thinking may prove to be the richest thinking possible.

Sleep Thinking and Dreaming

Abby had many dreams as a result of sleep thinking. She learned that by focusing on a single question, she instantly altered her dream repertoire and began to have dreams about her roommate Jan, someone whom she had never dreamed about before. She also learned that most of her dreams did not feel significant, even though on a superficial level they seemed to be communicating something about her problem. She knew intuitively that most of these dreams were incidental, not consequential. Only the rock concert dream felt like it had *thought* behind it, and that was the only dream Abby felt compelled to really consider.

Some people think that all dreams are important. Some people think that no dreams are important. The commonsense view, which is held by most people, is also the biologically accurate one: Most dreams are not informative, and only occasionally does a dream have something vital to tell us. The average dream is just a lively but meaningless hodgepodge of thoughts and impressions or a simple reminder about some fact about existence, such as "there is anxiety" or "there are dangers." For example, all people have recurrent anxiety dreams about being trapped or chased, about forgetting to do an important assignment or to show up at an important meeting, and so on. Such dreams may arise because we ate a richer meal than usual or because we have a pain in our side from a pulled muscle. They may simply be our "upset" dreams which return when we are upset or unwell, rather than a signal that we are anxious about something. In short, these dreams may be meaningless.

By contrast, some dreams are informative. They are answers to questions we have posed in or out of conscious awareness. Creative people, when they are incubating or working on a project, have dreams of this sort on a regular basis. For example, the author Isabel Allende explained in Naomi Epell's *Writers Dreaming*:

With House of the Spirits *I'd written the last fifteen pages more than ten times and I could never get it right. I couldn't get the tone. One night, at three o'clock in the morning, I woke up with a dream and I realized that the end of the book would be that the grandfather had died and the granddaughter is waiting for the dawn to bury him. So the epilogue has the tone of a person sitting beside her grandfather, who is dead, telling the story very simply. The dream gave me that.*

The fact that some dreams are meaningful and most aren't means that we have to be discriminating in our approach to our dreams, a little skeptical about their value, not too quick to find everything we dream fascinating, and aligned with our own powers of intuition. This is not hard to do. Once we get into the habit of focusing on some issue when we go to bed, as Abby did, then we'll begin to sense which of our dreams are irrelevant and which are part of the solution.

We go through this sorting process when we try to solve a problem of any kind, say, a tough math problem. During the time that we are searching for the answer, we discard many of the ideas that come to us without having to investigate them very much or even at all. They just feel wrong. The mathematician Pascal wrote about this discriminating ability in the following way (from *The Foundations of Science*):

To invent is to choose; but the word is perhaps not wholly accurate. It makes one think of a purchaser before whom are displayed a large number of samples, and who examines them, one after another, to make a choice. In mathematical invention the samples would be so numerous that a whole lifetime would not suffice to examine them. This is not the actual state of things. Never in the field of his consciousness do combinations appear to an inventive mathematician that are not really useful, except some that he rejects but which have to some extent the characteristics of useful combinations. All goes on as if the inventor were an examiner for the second degree who would only have to question the candidates who had passed a previous examination.

Only those dreams that feel as if they have passed a "previous examination" are worth our attention. Just as the mathematician discards more of his mathematical thoughts than he saves and does so without any special effort, so the practiced sleep thinker begins to discard dreams that do not have that relevant feel to them so as not to get bogged down in incessant dream analysis. As a colleague of mine told me, "I get certain anxiety dreams all the time. They really don't mean anything and I don't waste my time thinking about them. They're old news. Yes, I get anxious; yes, I have to live with anxiety; like I need those dreams to remind me!"

One of your first jobs is to enter into a new, more discriminating relationship with your dreams. Toward that end, here's your first exercise. I hope you'll take the time to try it.

I'd like you to start a dream journal. But this isn't a typical dream journal. In a typical dream journal, you record all of your dreams and attempt to analyze them. In this journal I'd like you to do the following:

1. Only record those dreams that feel meaningful. This will provide you with the opportunity to practice using your intuition and critical thinking skills to distinguish between dreams that are irrelevant and those that have thought behind them. To actually do this, you may have to start recording a dream and then decide while you're recording it that it doesn't feel particularly meaningful. After a few lines, you may find yourself saying, "Nope, I don't think so. Nothing here." So your dream journal may have many entries that end abruptly.

2. With those dreams that feel meaningful enough to record fully, rather than analyzing them in a "micro" way, trying to figure out the meaning of a skyscraper or a freight train, try instead to discern what question

or life issue the dream is attempting to answer. The same dream (e.g., you fighting with a coworker who refuses to hear anything you say, which makes you increasingly frustrated until you actually scream) may mean that you're having trouble speaking directly, which is one kind of issue, or that you're trapped in an unhealthy relationship, which is another issue, or that you're being eaten up by rage, which is a third issue. Only you can tell what the dream is really about, because you are the one who actually "lived" through it and can judge its details, resonance, and feeling tones. You are the only eyewitness to your dream. With each of these meaningful dreams, take the time to find out what the dream was really about and what it was trying to get at.

3. Start to make a list of the "life thread" questions or issues that emerge from your analysis of your meaningful dreams. There is no demand that you arrive at a perfect understanding of each dream or that you pinpoint just one issue that your dream is addressing. In the example I gave, you may not be able to conclude whether the dream is really about speaking more directly, getting out of a relationship, or working on your rage. That you can't choose among them means that each is a possibility, which is valuable information in its own right. So put all three down on your list, for future study and investigation. You can use any divided notebook for this dream analysis and for the other work of the sleep thinking program.

Why Do I Hate Openings?

Let's take a look at another example of how sleep thinking works.

Mary, an excellent painter, came to see me with a career-related concern. She had the feeling that she was sabotaging her career by refusing to do any networking. What particularly concerned her was her refusal to attend gallery openings, even though she understood that she needed to get to know gallery owners, collectors, and her fellow artists firsthand in order to sell her paintings. She felt frustrated, disappointed with herself, and at a loss about how to proceed.

She recounted her checkered history with regard to openings. Even though she hated cocktail party events, which made her anxious and offended her sensibilities, for a whole year she'd tried to put in appearances on a regular basis at openings that interested her. But after a glance at the show, a few bites of cheese, and a quick glass of wine, she'd rush right home. She never lasted more than 10 or 15 minutes, and she never talked to anyone who "mattered." She called these quick exits her "disappearing acts."

At first she thought that the problem had something to do with the paintings themselves. She usually didn't like them very much. But even when she liked them, she left just as quickly. Then she figured that it had something to do with the sexual dynamics at these openings; everyone seemed to be "hitting" on everyone else. But that didn't really bother her. Then it struck her that maybe "not knowing anybody" was the problem and that it might be better to come with a friend. So she tried bringing a friend, but that turned out even more poorly. She still wanted to leave after 10 minutes, but her friend didn't, which led to a fight and a month of estrangement.

But Mary didn't give up. She decided that at the next opening she would network, come hell or high water. At that opening, she picked a pleasant older woman out of the crowd and, after they'd chatted awhile, began explaining her work to her. The woman, very sweet and receptive, called her husband over to meet Mary. "Come here, dear, there's someone I want you to meet!" Mary began to explain to him how she used gold leaf in her painting process, which inspired him to interrupt her with a panning-for-gold story. This time Mary stayed much longer than usual, but when she got home, she found herself seriously depressed.

In counseling, Mary was invited to ask herself what disturbed her about openings. Rather than trying to pin down the answer, her goal was to generate a list of resonant questions. She came up with these six questions:

》 Why do I despise openings so much?
》 What am I hoping to get out of openings?
》 Is the question about the art I see or about the art I make?
》 If I feel so antagonistic toward gallery owners, collectors, and everyone else who shows up at openings, how will I ever exhibit or sell my paintings?
》 Do all gatherings make me anxious?
》 What am I hoping will happen at these openings? Do I expect to be discovered?

Generating this list felt very important to Mary. She understood that few people ever try such a thing. She herself certainly never had. Most of us are too busy, prideful, stubborn, and anxious to chat with ourselves about anything.

When she went over the list a second time, the last question struck home. It felt as if a knife had been twisted in her stomach. She gave herself a version of that question to sleep think: Am I such an idiot that I expect to be discovered at openings of other artists' paintings? That night she dreamt that she was passing out postcards printed with a likeness of a painting that she hadn't yet painted but that was certainly one of her own. She watched herself pass out the postcards at a crowded gallery opening; she was smiling, shaking hands, and saying to each person, "Have a nice day!"

The dream woke her up. After replaying it in her mind, she felt compelled to ask herself this question: Have I never tried to sell myself? Is it that simple? Should I be trying harder to acquire representation?

Mary felt agitated after this realization, but not upset. That night she took a new question to bed to sleep think: Have I never really tried to sell myself? Though she didn't remember her dreams the next morning, she had the sense that an answer had come to her.

At the same time, she had the feeling that she'd never been closer to her own creative process. She woke up really wanting to paint. But she realized that a new injunction was at work in her psyche. What she heard herself saying was, "Sell before you paint!" Over coffee that morning, she wrote up the first business plan of her life. Then she painted all afternoon, relieved to see that thinking about business hadn't ruined her creativity.

Over the next several months, we worked on her presentation skills, her anxiety about discussing her work, her hatred of "playing the gallery games," and other obstacles to successfully connecting in the marketplace. She took new issues to bed to sleep think, came up with answers, and could feel herself growing into a more savvy artist.

At the same time—and to her, the most surprising result of all—her painting style deepened. It seemed that by paying attention to the needs of her painting career, she was at the same time causing herself to pay better attention to the needs of her paintings.

Within a year, she had her first show arranged. When it went up, it drew more attention than most first shows do, because of her willingness to go the extra mile to publicize it and because she took the time to sleep think the question: How can I make this show a great success? (( ))

Learning the Steps of the Sleep Thinking Program

The key elements of the sleep thinking program are awareness, desire, engagement, and surrender. Mary, the painter I described in the last chapter, grew aware of what was going on in her personality, manifested a real desire to make changes, engaged with each new question as it arose, and surrendered herself each night to learning about her own life. We'll look at each of these four elements in turn as we examine the steps of the sleep thinking program. But to begin with I want to communicate the following point: that *any* honorable attempt you make at self-inquiry and sleep thinking will net you results.

For many of us, so much is going on that we can't dissect our lives in a neat way or come up with a single problem that stands out from all the rest. Often, we just feel a lack or a hole in our life, without being able to articulate what that hole or lack represents. Or maybe we have so many personality changes to make—becoming more confident, more self-trusting, more disciplined, and so on—that no single change sticks out or seems more important than the others. Very often we can't seem to isolate or articulate a single "thing" to work on.

Consider Tom. When Tom hit 40, his wife shocked him by suddenly informing him that she was leaving him and filing for divorce. The subsequent divorce process was drawn out, bitter, and hurt like nothing Tom had experienced before. His two sons, in their early teens at the time, took the breakup as hard as he did and went from being average-to-good students to almost failing. It took Tom five years to get back on his feet and feel even a little bit normal.

At 46, he remarried and had two children with his second wife. But he saw his wife and daughters very little because he made it a point to climb the ladder at work and, therefore, spent more and more time there. He stayed late almost every night and often slept all day Saturday to deal with his exhaustion. He knew in a corner of his mind that he was avoiding life and not really living it, but there didn't seem to be anything he could do to turn matters around.

As he approached 60, he realized that he could retire soon and get two-thirds of his salary for life, an amount that would allow for a comfortable retirement. But his wife, 10 years his junior, still wanted to work as a pediatric nurse, and their two daughters were only ten and twelve. He couldn't see sitting at home, doing nothing, while everyone else in the house went about their business. Furthermore, the thought of not working put him into a panic. So instead of slowing down, he worked harder than ever before.

He had the suspicion that he couldn't face retirement because, with that much time on his hands, he would start to experience the loneliness he felt—the loneliness he had always felt—and all the hurt that remained from the divorce, though already almost 20 years old. But he kept these suspicions to himself and publicly asserted that he was too young to retire and that everything at work would fall apart if he left.

It was at this point that Tom started the sleep thinking program.

The first sleep thinking question he posed to himself was the general, but appropriate, What's going on in my life? He had a series of strange dreams that made no sense to him, having to do with space cities and adventures that felt right out of an Indiana Jones movie. Some of these dreams were exhilarating and some nightmarish, but none felt informative.

But it excited him to be having such vivid dreams, and after about two weeks of recording his dreams—but only in part, since none of them felt truly meaningful—he decided "out of the blue" to change his question from What's going on in my life? to What hurts so much? His dreams changed abruptly, as if he had switched channels. Instead of tuning in to the science fiction channel, he seemed to have switched to *Lifetime* and television for women. He began dreaming about small towns and people going about their business. There were small dramas about divorced men and women going on first dates and feeling awkward and embarrassed. Unlike his science fiction dreams, these dreams felt meaningful, and he recorded them in detail. But he had no idea what they signified. Those about an "endless summer" of softball games and lake swimming felt the most meaningful of all, yet Tom couldn't say what these dreams were getting at.

No "answer" came to him, and he wasn't really sure that he'd even landed on the right question. But on the Thanksgiving before his 60th birthday, with his whole family gathered at his house for dinner, his grandson, his oldest boy's son, made a passing remark. He mentioned that his history teacher was looking for parent volunteers to help aboard the *Barclay*, a three-masted schooner that the state had purchased to teach high school students about navigation and practical seamanship. Tom, who had never volunteered at his children's school—not even once—knew all of a sudden that his "endless summer" dreams had primed him for exactly this moment. He decided not only that he *would* volunteer but also that he *had to* volunteer.

He loved the training given to new volunteers and soon found himself spending every spare minute reading about schooners and the sea, a subject about which he knew next to nothing. In a few short months, he acquired a considerable understanding of schooner lore and seamanship. Best of all, his time aboard ship with these high school students, first in a peripheral capacity, helping out, but then more and more as a mentor and teacher, melted some glacial ice in his heart. He loved the ship, and he loved his time with these young people.

He continued reading voraciously, took a pair of working cruises on three-masted schooners, joined an Internet chat group, and found his imagination awakening. Then one day, reading an out-of-print book about 19th-century schooner travel, he came upon a brief description of an astounding voyage. It struck him that he wanted to learn more about this wild adventure and maybe even write a book about it. He began researching on the Internet, used interlibrary loan services to get his hands on a few relevant books, and then took a trip to a maritime library in South Carolina to look at the period documents collected there.

Tom is now two years into his retirement. Three days a week he researches and writes his book, whose working title is *The Voyage of the* Charlotte Anne. Two days a week he teaches teenagers on the *Barclay*, learning more about schooners and the sea each time he goes aboard and never failing to relish his hours in the company of these young people. His relationship with his young daughters is different, too. He is beginning to know them. Sometimes the three of them find themselves laughing together, about someone at school who dyed her hair purple or got a second nose ring. People tell Tom that retirement seems to be agreeing with him, and he can only nod and smile.

Would Tom have seized the opportunity to volunteer if he hadn't been working the sleep thinking program? Perhaps. But he had dramatically increased his odds of opening up to new possibilities by honestly trying to ask and answer some questions about his life. The answer never came to him directly, and he couldn't even say that he'd landed on the right question. But still the process of sleep thinking readied him to learn from life what he needed to know just as soon as the opportunity presented itself.

Q. *Has there been much scientific work done on sleep thinking yet?*

No. It appears it will be some time before researchers begin asking questions such as What sort of *thinking* goes on at night? and How can we improve our ability to think while we sleep? The prejudice against the idea that we engage in "real" thinking while we sleep is nicely captured in the following paragraph from a standard psychology text, Peter Gray's *Psychology* (3rd edition):

When people are awakened during slow-wave sleep, they report some sort of mental activity just before awakening in roughly half of the cases. Such reports are usually not of true dreams but of sleep thought, which lacks the vivid sensory and motor hallucinations of true dreams and is more akin to daytime thinking. Often the subject of sleep thought is some problem that had been of concern during the day. For example, a student who had been cramming for a math exam might report working on a calculus problem while sleeping. The main difference between sleep thought and daytime thought is that the former is usually ineffective.

But Alexander Borbely in *Secrets of Sleep* reminds us that the ancients understood some important things that researchers today are unprepared to accept:

In Eastern philosophies and religions sleep has sometimes been depicted as the real and true human state, in which the universe and the individual are at one. The Chinese philosopher Chuang-tzu (300 B.C.) wrote, "Everything is one: during sleep the soul, undistracted, is absorbed into this unity; when awake, distracted, it sees many things and hence far less." In a passage in the ancient Indian philosophical texts of the Upanishads, deep sleep and the real self are connected: "Now when one is thus sound asleep, composed, serene, and knows no dream, that is the Self (Atman), that is the immortal, the fearless, that is Brahma."

What Sleep Thinking Can Do for You

The sleep thinking program can help you with the following:

》 It can help you to change something about your personality. Maybe you want to become more disciplined, more self-trusting, more assertive, or more open. Sleep thinking can help if there's a personality change of any sort that you want to make, even if you can't articulate the nature of the change and only know that you want to be "different."

》 It can help you to alter your relationship to work, feel less stress there, make progress up the ladder, change jobs or careers, become self-employed, work smarter, handle difficult people at your job more effectively, or in any way improve the quality of your work life.

》 It can help you to lose weight, quit smoking, gain sobriety, stop your drug use, deal with compulsive spending or compulsive Internet use, or change any pattern of behavior whose intertwined social, psychological, and biological roots make it painfully hard to combat.

》 It can help you to improve your relationships (both your personal and your professional ones), learn how to communicate more effectively, be more loving, react less critically or angrily to other people's behaviors, let go of grudges more quickly, or improve some other aspect of your relational life.

)) It can help you to solve a practical problem (such as whether or not to buy earthquake insurance or switch from one HMO to another), how to manage your time more effectively, or handle any one of the other countless problems that pepper our lives.

)) If can help you to solve an intellectual problem of the sort that arises in the course of your work as a scientist, inventor, business person, or artist, problems such as coming up with new products, evaluating the effectiveness of your novel, determining the best solvent to use to safely eliminate waste materials in a production process, or calculating what points to make for an effective jury summation.

)) It can help you to work more deeply and effectively on a creative project like a novel, painting, play, story, symphony, scientific theory, professional article, workshop presentation, or any other enterprise that requires that you access your creative potential.

)) It can help you to solve some mental health problem (such as depression or anxiety), reduce the stress in your life, learn some stress management skills, deal with psychological issues (such as mental confusion, obsessive thinking, or self-sabotaging behaviors), or improve anything in the realm of the psychological.

)) It can help you to articulate for yourself what spirituality means, determine what activities and practices feel soulful, envision your personal spiritual path, reconcile the secular and the spiritual, or find a way to be an atheist or an agnostic and also a spiritual being.

》 It can help you to solve problems as simple as whether or not to install French doors to the patio or as complex as whether or not to give up your salaried job and start a home business. There is nothing in your life that your own brain can't be invited to think about at night while you sleep. If your brain is invited, it will provide you with answers and openings to understanding—sometimes in dreams and sometimes not in dreams.

In a previous exercise you set aside a section of your sleep thinking journal to record dreams and assess their meaningfulness. Now I'd like you to start another section and begin recording issues of importance to you that you may want to solve or better understand through sleep thinking. Use the following 10 categories and leave a couple of pages of space for each one. As you read along and begin to think about the important issues in your life, note them in the appropriate categories. Life is so complex that it isn't easy to know whether your unhappiness at work, say, is precisely a personality issue, a work issue, or a mental health issue, so just record such problems in all three categories.

Here are the 10 categories. You can also create any other categories that feel pertinent.

1. Personality

2. Work issues

3. Behavior patterns

4. Relationships

5. Practical problems

6. Intellectual problems

7. Creative projects

8. Mental health

9. Spiritual health

10. Other issues or problems

The best-known and most frequently repeated examples of sleep thinking have to do with solving intellectual problems during sleep. If you've read books on dream work, you're probably quite familiar with some of the famous examples of well-known scientists, inventors, and artists who had solutions to their intellectual problems arrive at night. Here are a few examples:

)) In 1903 the German physiologist Otto Loewi came up with a new theory about the chemical transmission of nerve impulses. But it wasn't until 17 years later that the experiment to prove his theory came to him. In 1920, he had the following experience:

The night before Easter Sunday I awoke, turned on the light, and jotted down a few notes on a slip of paper. Then I fell asleep again. It occurred to me at six o'clock in the morning that during the night I had written down something important, but I was unable to decipher the scrawl. The next night, at three o'clock in the morning, the idea returned. I got up immediately, went to the laboratory, and performed a simple experiment on a frog heart according to that nocturnal design. Its results became the foundation of the theory of the chemical transmission of the nervous impulse.

» The German chemist Friedrich Auguste Kekule spent years puzzling over the chemical structure of benzene without unraveling its mystery. Then one night he fell asleep in his armchair. He recalled what happened next:

I dozed off and atoms danced before my eyes. I saw long rows of atoms, densely joined, contorting and turning like snakes; then one of the snakes took hold of its own tail and whirled derisively before my eyes. I woke up as though struck by lightning and spent the rest of the night working out the consequences.

» In the introduction to *Dreamtime and Dreamwork*, we learn about the invention of the sewing machine:

In 1844 the inventor Elias Howe dreamed that a savage king ordered his execution because he had not been able to perfect a lockstitch sewing machine. As the warriors' spears approached his body, Howe observed that they had eye-shaped holes near their heads. Awakening, Howe went to his laboratory and whittled a model of the needle, placing the hole near the tip, thus bringing his efforts of several years to a successful conclusion.

» Gayle Delaney recounted in *Personal and Professional Problem Solving in Dreams*:

W. B. Cannon, one of America's greatest physiologists, wrote that awakenings in the middle of the night led him to new theories and designs for inventions, such as his device for obtaining an automatically written record of the clotting of blood. As a child he would purposely "sleep on" problems in algebra and on how he might repair broken toys. Cannon wrote further that "as a matter of routine I have long trusted uncon- scious processes to serve me—for example, when I have had to prepare a public address. I would gather points for the address and write them down in a rough outline. Within the next few nights I would have sudden spells of awakening, with an onrush of illustrative instances, pertinent phrases, and fresh ideas related to those already listed."

》 The mystery writer Sue Grafton explained the following in *Writers Dreaming*:

I reach a point in many of my books, when I'm heavily engaged in the process of writing, where I have a problem that I can't solve. As I go to sleep I give myself the suggestion that a solution will come. I know that I will awaken and a solution will be there. For instance, I was working on a novel called B is for Burglar. *I had gotten writer's block. I sat at my desk for weeks. Then one night in the wee hours of the morning I woke up and a little voice said, "I know how to make the story work." I suddenly understood that I was to take the same story and tell it from a different angle. That didn't come out of a dream per se but it came out of the same state that does create our dreams."*

Many of us accomplish this kind of problem solving when we sleep. Holly Reed, president of the East Bay chapter of California Marriage and Family Therapists, explained this to me:

I've solved many problems, studied for tests, written letters, written lengthy papers for school, and even completed my dissertation while asleep! I've been doing this since high school. I've always been a successful student and mostly maintained a 3.7–4.0 g.p.a. I just fall asleep thinking about whatever I'm working on and the answers or word or phrases come to me in the night. I've tried to explain this method to people and they usually laugh and don't believe it's possible. But I passed both Marriage and Family Therapists written and oral tests on the first try using this method.

Solving intellectual problems, writing papers, and studying for tests are only a few of the uses to which you can put sleep thinking. At least as important is the way you can use the sleep thinking program to investigate any emotional, psychological, relational, or spiritual problems that arise in your life. For example, take the case of Jodie.

Jodie was a 31-year-old nurse who enjoyed her job and happened at the moment to be single. What troubled her was her estrangement from her older sister, Renee, whose birthday was just a month away. As Renee's birthday approached, Jodie was painfully reminded of the fact that they hadn't spoken for 10 months, even though before that they would speak every couple of weeks. What had happened? Jodie thought back to the last time they were together the previous Christmas.

Jodie had been dating a new man, Mark, for a few weeks. She'd brought Mark to the family Christmas party and introduced him to everyone. About a week later, she and Renee were speaking on the phone, and Renee mentioned that Mark had been drinking a lot at the party. Renee wondered if Mark had a problem. Jodie became furious with Renee for mentioning Mark's drinking and told Renee that she needed to mind her own business.

As Renee's birthday approached, Jodie still couldn't figure out why she had gotten so angry and why she still felt so angry about it. Thinking about the situation, Jodie realized that Renee was only trying to help. In fact, Jodie and Mark *did* break up; Jodie saw pretty quickly that there were many things wrong with him, including his drinking.

To try to figure out why she was still angry with her sister, Jodie compiled the following list of questions to sleep think:

» Why am I still so angry at Renee?
» Why did I become so angry in the first place, if Renee was only trying to help?
» What can I do to let go of this anger and reconcile with Renee?
» How can I start the communication ball rolling between us?
» What can I do to make my relationship with Renee work?

Jodie chose the last question to sleep think, but after a week, she hadn't seen any results. She looked over her list and decided that it might be easier if she started at a different point. So she changed her sleep thinking question to Why did I become so angry in the first place, if Renee was only trying to help?

It took Jodie a few nights to get to the point where she could recite her question without feeling any residual anger. She knew that she had to say the question as calmly as she could so that it was more like a meditation than an accusation. If she could get to the point where her mind was reasonably calm, she would have much better luck sleep thinking. After about a week, Jodie was able to say her question a little more gently, and soon thereafter, she began to see results.

One night in her sleep she heard her mother's voice saying, "You cannot see Tim ever again, young lady!" She recognized her mother's voice, even though there was no dream or visual images involved. She thought about the incident referred to in her sleep. When Jodie was a teenager, her mother forbade her from going out with Tim, a very nice young man who was older than Jodie by four years. She hated her mom for forbidding her to see Tim and almost ran away with him just to spite the family.

Not sure what to make of this sleep thought, Jodie continued with her question. Two nights later she heard the same thing, only this time her mother said, "You cannot see Mark ever again, young lady!" Jodie woke up, startled, realizing that she heard Mark's name instead of Tim's. She also suddenly understood that she'd become furious with Renee because it felt as if Renee had acted as their mother had when Jodie was a teenager.

Jodie reflected on her sleep thoughts. It made sense to her that she must be taking out a lot of the anger she felt toward her mother on her older sister. Could she start to let go of her anger now that her sleep thoughts had helped her see the difference between the actions of her mother and those of Renee? Her mother had laid down the law; more than that, she'd been mean-spirited and unfair. Renee, on the other hand, had only made some observations. Maybe she should have kept them to herself, but, by the same token, maybe Jodie could finally forgive her.

The very next day Jodie called Renee and made up with her. She didn't precisely apologize, because she still wasn't sure that Renee was blameless in the interaction. Instead of apologizing, Jodie just chatted in a light-hearted way about looking forward to Renee's birthday and getting together with her. Renee took the cue and agreed that it would be great to see her little sister. Neither of them brought up Mark or their unfortunate Christmas conversation.

The Steps of the Sleep Thinking Program

Here are the 18 steps that comprise the sleep thinking program. In subsequent sections, we'll look at each one in detail.

Step 1. Commit to self-awareness. First you need a willingness to think about what's going on in your life. Freud and the psychoanalysts were right to say that we're defended against knowing ourselves, and Jung and the depth psychologists were right to propose the idea of blind spots, those areas of our life that we have trouble spotting. The first step of the sleep thinking program is to dispute your natural tendency to avoid knowing yourself.

Step 2. Affirm your desire to answer your own questions. When you say, "I want to know why I'm doing such and such and what I can do to change it," you're injecting a dose of life-affirming optimism into your system. You're also awakening your brain, which operates at only a percentage of its power when it has no tricky questions to contemplate.

Step 3. Brainstorm current issues and questions. The 15 minutes that it takes to sit with yourself and generate a "master list" of current issues and questions is a tremendous use of your time and an activity that breaks through your defenses. Your brain begins to make important connections, ones that it will continue to play with and work on while you sleep.

Step 4. Identify particular issues and questions to focus on. It's possible to sleep think without a particular issue or question in mind but it's more productive to identify issues that concern you. Then ask yourself questions about them and select one question from your list to use as your sleep thinking prompt.

Step 5. Manage anxiety. One of the great impediments to thinking is anxiety. When you're too anxious you can forget your own telephone number or find the simplest mental calculations impossible to do. Since thinking about your problems provokes a great deal of anxiety, learning effective anxiety management strategies is a vital part of the sleep thinking program.

Step 6. Refashion bedtime so that you're prepared to sleep think. Your bedtime habits, especially your habits of mind, affect how well you sleep think. Imagine going into a chemistry test drunk, exhausted, stressed out about your failing marriage, unprepared for the test, and unwilling to think about chemistry. This is not a recipe for success. How you approach sleep will affect how productively you sleep think.

Step 7. Fall asleep with a wonder, not a worry. When you go to sleep worrying, you're inviting anxiety dreams—or even nightmares—rather than sleep thought. An important part of the sleep thinking program is learning how to enter sleep more meditatively, gently wondering about your sleep thinking question rather than worrying about some life stressor. When you master this change, you'll also have mastered a useful stress reduction technique.

Step 8. Surrender to nighttime brain work. It's human nature both to want to know and not want to know what's going on in your life. Genuine curiosity and real denial both are a part of our make-up. So you have to pay attention to whether you're letting your brain think freely as you sleep or whether you're restricting it with silent injunctions. If such injunctions are in place, you'll want to learn how to exorcise them.

Step 9. If your thoughts awaken you, arise during the night to record them. Sleep thinking produces thought. The brain may deliver up that thought in dreams or not in dreams, in the morning when you awake, or insistently in the middle of the night. People are not used to accepting their own night thoughts; they may find them annoying and disturbing or even frightening. So one of the tasks of the sleep thinking program is to learn to accept that you may be awakened at night by your thoughts. Then your job is to get up and record them.

Step 10. Spend time first thing each morning processing night thoughts. A crucial element of the sleep thinking program is allowing time first thing each morning for thoughts that may have been generated during the night to make themselves known to you. If you awake and immediately start to worry about your day, you're silencing your sleep thoughts. So a vital part of the sleep thinking program is making a commitment to spend a little time—as few as 10 minutes—as soon as you awaken to allow your brain to bring forth answers that it may have found.

Step 11. Make sense of the information you receive. Sometimes your sleep thoughts will be very clear to you; you will know exactly what they mean and exactly what you're supposed to do with them. You go right to the laboratory, for example, and launch an effective experiment or right to work and say the perfect thing to resolve a conflict between two employees. But just as often the information isn't obvious; it feels more like tantalizing clues that must be unraveled if you're to solve the mystery. Part of the sleep thinking program is learning how to accomplish the detective work that will be required of you.

Step 12. Make use of the information you receive. What you learn from your sleep thinking needs to be applied to your life problems, intellectual problems, or creative problems in order to prove useful. You may learn that to change course at work you have to bring new confidence to the job, but you may have a lot of thinking to do in order to figure out how you'll go about acting more confidently. You may learn that the novel you're writing requires a new antagonist, but there may be considerable work left to do before you effectively craft that new character. Sleep thinking gives you answers, but it also presents you with new work.

Step 13. Plan for any necessary work or change. Planning is an important part of the sleep thinking program. The plan you make can be very simple—as simple as identifying two or three steps you mean to take to make a change or do the work suggested by your sleep thoughts. But you'll find that even the simplest plan is valuable and can make all the difference between reaching or not reaching your goals.

Step 14. Accomplish the work or make the changes. It's one thing to plan for change and another thing to actually make the change. One goal of the sleep thinking program is that you gain insight into your problems. But another important goal is that you solve those problems by accomplishing the needed work and making the necessary changes. No weight is lost by planning alone, no relationship is improved by planning alone, and no play is staged by planning alone. Sleep thinkers are also doers who become expert at taking effective action.

Step 15. Keep track of your progress. In your sleep thinking journal you'll be making many kinds of entries. You'll record meaningful dreams, issues that are present in your life, sleep thoughts, plans for change, and so on. You'll also want to keep track of your progress as you work to solve your problems. This ongoing self-analysis serves as a record of your progress and alerts you to any new or additional work that may be needed.

Step 16. Sleep think new issues and questions. Some issues may not get resolved easily, which may force you to sleep think them in new and different ways. Some will get resolved completely, but then another problem requiring some sleep thinking attention will rear its head. You may also discover in the course of keeping your sleep thinking journal and engaging in ongoing self-reflection that new avenues open up that are worthwhile to pursue. Sleep thinking is a lifelong self-help strategy.

Step 17. Bring sleep thinking fundamentals to your daytime thinking. Many of the things you learn in the sleep thinking program can be effectively applied to your thinking processes while you're awake. You can begin to "catnap" think as you take a moment right in the middle of your busy day to frame a question, present it to yourself as a wonder, and surrender to your natural ability to problem solve. In this way, you turn the sleep thinking program into a complete problem-solving program, increasing not only your sleep thinking skills but also all of your critical thinking skills.

Step 18. Live an examined life. Sleep thinking is your brain working effectively while you sleep. But for it to work effectively, it has to be pointed in the right direction. You can invite your brain to solve hard intellectual problems, and it will do so, but that's just one direction in which to point it. If you use sleep thinking only for solving intellectual problems, you'll miss out in your personal life. The sleep thinking program emphasizes living an examined life, one in which you can learn for yourself through self-inquiry how to relate, how to be intimate, how to be mentally healthy, how to be good, and how to be happy.

These may look like a lot of steps, but they're as straightforward as the steps in a recipe, which may look daunting in a cookbook but can be child's play to follow once you get started. In fact, some of these steps are difficult. Dealing with anxiety or coming to grips with psychological defenses, for example, can be lifelong challenges, but *any* work you do on them will improve your life dramatically.

$Q.$ *I'm still not sure I get it. What is sleep thinking?*

Sleep thinking is nothing more than your natural ability to think while you sleep. This is a very clear sentence, and yet at the heart of it is something mysterious.

Most people don't understand how to take charge of their own thoughts. They have the sense that thoughts come to them, not that they are doing the thinking. They don't have the experience of working with their thoughts in the kind of active, concerted way that it takes to produce a novel, a battle plan, a business plan, a scientific theory, or a better mousetrap. So when I say that the sleep thinking program helps you use—even maximize— your natural ability to think, what I am really saying is *that you are in charge of your own thinking*. One of the ways you can take charge of your thoughts is by inviting your brain to work at night in your behalf.

You have a natural ability to think. Your brain has lots of other vital things to do, such as monitoring your breathing, recognizing images, and alerting you to danger. But it is also terrific at making the connections we call thinking, connecting the idea of measurement with the idea of length and allowing us to say the profound and quite amazing, "I need a yard of fabric, please." Thinking is really a startling power, yet we take it for granted and rarely bother to hone it. How often have you said to yourself, "I think I'll devote a little time to thinking"? Sleep thinking is a great way to take that time.

What I'm articulating is a program for using that natural ability you were born with in ways that you may not have considered before. I hope the phrase *I'll sleep on it* already has new meaning for you. ((•))

3

CHAPTER

Zeroing In on Problems

In this chapter we'll examine the first four steps of the sleep thinking program:

Step 1. Commit to self-awareness.

Step 2. Affirm your desire to answer your own questions.

Step 3. Brainstorm current issues and questions.

Step 4. Identify particular issues and questions to focus on.

You can get started with your own sleep thinking efforts right away just by reminding yourself that your brain is your ally and that it can think at night. If you go to bed with a question in mind, as Abby did when she wondered if she should continue rooming with Jan, or as Mary did when she wondered what she hated about gallery openings, you'll be putting your brain on notice that it should sleep think. And it will. But if you make the extra effort to follow the steps of the program in a systematic way, you'll increase your odds of getting answers.

Commit to Self-Awareness

How well do you know yourself? If you're like most people, the answer is, Not well enough. We are built with an ability to know ourselves, but we are also built with a defensive structure that causes us to turn a blind eye to the truth about our motives, our circumstances, and our own personality. Following are some areas in which we commonly lack self-awareness:

1. *Our anxieties.* We're usually well aware that certain things make us anxious, like speaking in public, flying, or getting a root canal. But we're usually much less aware or even entirely unaware of the many other sources of anxiety in our life. Raised voices, feeling rushed, finding ourselves with a overlong to-do list, having a conversation with our child about school, or chatting with our elderly dad about his financial situation can fill us with anxiety. One of the goals of the sleep thinking program is to transform you into someone who recognizes how anxiety manifests itself in your life and who learns how to deal with it simply and effectively.

2. *Our habits.* We are all pretty much aware of those habits we'd like to change—habits such as smoking, eating compulsively, abusing alcohol, not following through on our resolutions, not appropriately asserting ourselves, and so on. What we have much less clarity about is how hard it is to change a habit. Because of our tendency toward wishful thinking, we hold to the dream that breaking our bad habits really isn't so hard, and then put off doing anything about them. We tell

ourselves that tomorrow we'll be able to take control and stop our drinking or do a better job of asserting ourselves. It's vitally important that we grow aware of how hard it is to break a habit, because until we surrender to that truth and understand how much is required of us to really change, we remain in a fantasy world with all of our bad habits still firmly in place.

3. *Our unmet dreams.* Because they're so painful to think about, we often remove from conscious awareness our thoughts and feelings about those dreams we used to hold that haven't come true. Maybe we hoped to get an undergraduate or a graduate degree, go into a certain career, have a family, work for ourselves, do creative work, be in a loving, intimate relationship, live in Paris or New York, or grow up to be taller, more beautiful, more handsome, or more athletic. Even if some of our dreams do come true, there always seem to be other dreams that haven't and don't look like they will. But some of them may still come true, if we're willing to think about them. And whether they will or won't, banishing them from awareness causes blind spots and prevents us from understanding our own motives and actions. Opening to an understanding of our unmet dreams is another area of self-knowledge that we accomplish much too rarely.

4. *Our faults.* Even if we regularly beat ourselves up about our faults, we still have a hard time naming them, thinking about them, and really owning them.

5. *Discipline.* Because we manage to get a certain number of things done, we credit ourselves with a reasonable amount of discipline. But we rarely want to examine how little discipline we're employing in other, often more important areas of our life.

6. *Self-interest.* Maybe it's natural that we're self-interested and just plain selfish creatures, but we often have trouble admitting that we've acted selfishly or that we're driven by

such "base" motives. Have you ever heard an adult admit to another adult, "That was selfish of me"?

7. *Revenge.* Because we're more thin-skinned than we like to admit and because we can be wounded by even the mildest criticism, we tend to brood and waste time dreaming up revenge fantasies. If we had more self-awareness, we'd simply dismiss the criticism that made no sense and make use of the criticism that applied.

What does it feel like to examine one of these areas? For most of us, it feels pretty bad, verging on terrible. It feels so bad because it threatens our self-concept and our self-esteem. To learn something negative about ourselves feels dangerous; we fear that we may be broken apart by the news. The same person who can skydive or enter a burning building to rescue children has his or her courage taxed when it comes to looking in the mirror. Even when there actually isn't anything negative there, the fear that there might be can paralyze us and prevent us from taking a peek.

I see this all the time with the adult college students I teach, many of whom are firefighters and police officers and actually do run into burning buildings, confront armed robbers, and do other brave things. Part of the reason they've put off returning to college to get their undergraduate degree is that 20 years before they failed at college, and during that intervening time, it felt too dangerous to think about what might have provoked that failure. Instead of looking in the mirror and realizing that they'd been a little too immature, too disinterested in college, or too taxed by working and going to school simultaneously, they instead are overly self-critical and call themselves names like "idiot" and "failure."

Those self-labels breed fear and doubt. They fear that their writing skills are too poor, that they're too undisciplined to write papers, or that they're not intellectually "up to snuff" to do college-level work. It turns out that none of this is true. If they could have looked in the mirror a little sooner and said to themselves, "I'm scared and I have my doubts about myself, but I'm going to give college another try anyway," they might have avoided two decades of self-chastisement and unmet dreams.

Therapists learn that they have to be *very* careful about pointing out what they see going on in their clients' lives. Adept therapists, by the way they frame their observations, by their manner and tone of voice, and by the way they join with clients so that the messages they deliver feel empathic and not critical, can speak about what they see without having their clients drop out of therapy. But even adept therapists know that they have to be very careful and that they can only say so much, because people tend to get wounded very easily; it is very hard for us to hear about our flaws and faults.

Our human defenses and frailties make it difficult to sleep think solutions to problems. If you're blaming your boss for being too demanding when in fact the problem is that you hate your job and are always finding ways to steal a little time off, if you haven't really processed all the effects of an early trauma, if you don't appreciate how critical or gruff you are, if, in short, you have trouble seeing to what extent you are part of the difficulty, it is very hard to sleep think solutions to the problems you face. Your own brain knows not to deliver up the truth, because it knows that you don't want the truth.

If you're brave enough to do this exercise, you'll gain more than you can imagine. Try the following exercise. Write about a page in answer to each of the following questions:

1. What don't I want to know about myself?

2. Would it be so bad if I revealed my own secrets to myself?

I'd like you to commit to better self-awareness. You'll live a richer life if you understand your own motives and your own personality. You'll also profit more from the sleep thinking program if your brain has the unambiguous message that it can think about anything and everything, without restrictions or injunctions. A defended brain is an enslaved brain. Free yours.

Tonight, sleep think on the following question: What don't I want to know about myself? Feel open to this question and ready to accept your own truth. You may be wondering how I can ask you to sleep think before I present all 18 steps. The answer is that no steps are really necessary. They are just aids to help you effectively use your natural ability to think while you sleep. The gist of sleep thinking is that if you go to bed thinking about some question that you really want answered, sooner or later you will get an answer. That is the long and the short of it. So there's no reason why you can't begin sleep thinking right away, if you're willing and open to the process. In the morning, spend some time sitting quietly with your journal. Ask yourself the question again, think about it, and write down your thoughts.

Affirm Your Desire to Answer Your Own Questions

A great mathematician solves his math problems because he's studied mathematics and, more importantly, because he's willed himself to apply all of his native intelligence to the task of solving math problems. A great novelist arrives at her strongest characters and her most effective plot because she's read a lot of literature and, more importantly, because she's willed herself to understand the demands of fiction writing. We solve our life problems not just by living life but also by willing ourselves to make use of our experiences in the service of understanding our own motives and personality. In order to know, we have to want to know.

When we commit to self-awareness, we will ourselves to question our actions, motives, intentions, strategies, and even our very personality. This is as it should be. We should engage in this inquiry, because we can learn so much from it. If we dare to answer even the apparently simplest questions, we can provide ourselves with a wealth of information. For instance, I once asked some high school students who were active in high school theatricals and who hoped to go on to a life in the theater the following simple question: What do you find most difficult about being a young theater artist? Here are some of their replies:

Jim: "Self-consciousness. The idea that many teenagers have that you must fit into some kind of mold to 'be cool' makes it hard and sometimes embarrassing to express yourself truly."

Barbara: "I get highly disappointed when I get turned down for a role. I know it's a learning experience, but it's hard to be told no."

Melanie: "Stage fright and not being able to think before doing improvisation."

Alex: "Conflicting advice. You're brought up being told to shut up and to keep your emotions inside, and you teach yourself to be invulnerable, lest you get hurt, but now you are supposed to spill your insides to the world."

Rachel: "The constant judgment of your own 'talent' as an actor and whether you are talented enough to make the theater a career."

Melvin: "Young people in general don't get very much respect. And on the same note, actors in general don't get very much respect. So put both together, and you get us."

Jessica: "There are so many actors in our school alone, and they are all so talented I find it hard to get parts."

Brian: "There are a lot of kids who get primped by mothers 24 hours a day and show up at auditions with a fancy resume. And then there are those (like me) who must make it on their own."

Lois: "Taking risks, expressing my ideas, just going for it, even though judgment of me may come out of it."

Even such a simple question as this one elicits important information—and different information in each case. Each answer suggests issues in these young persons' lives and worthwhile avenues to pursue. With Melanie, I might want to work directly on stage fright. With Alex, I'd want to focus on expressing emotions. With Brian, I'd hope to help him ventilate his anger about not getting any career help from his family. With Rachel, I'd hope to turn around her low self-esteem suggested by her self-characterization that she doesn't possess talent. And so on.

Virtually any simple, direct, pertinent question will garner you useful information. But you have to want to ask it. You have to say to yourself, "I want to know." You have to let go of the fear that the answer will be too depressing or disastrous. You have to let go of the worry that there's no hope. Try it right now. Say "I want to know." Say it out loud. Try all of these variations:

》 I want to know what's up.
》 I want to know what to do.
》 I want to know how I'm part of the problem.
》 I want to know my own personality.
》 I want to know everything I need to know.

Consider the following example. Becca is a 19-year-old college student who's about to start her sophomore year. She's taken several classes that have put her on track to declare a major in either biology or English, both of which interest her. But she has no idea which one to choose, nor can she actually picture what sort of life either one would offer her. What would she do with an undergraduate degree in English or with one in biology? It isn't just that she can't decide what she wants to do; it's that she can't even imagine how she might go about deciding. And shortly, she must declare her major.

She also has issues in the area of dating. She's been out on several dates in the past few months but doesn't feel as though any of those relationships had a chance of working. She especially liked John, but after a few dates, she found an insignificant fault with him and broke off the relationship. She wonders whether she's in some kind of self-sabotaging mode, refusing to look at her future and also refusing to look at her relationships with men.

Becca feels that there are a lot of things in her life that she can't control anymore, nor can she seem to make decisions or plans for her future. This is entirely natural for a person of Becca's age, but still it's a painful and confusing situation. Many young people in Becca's circumstance make decisions—from choosing a profession that isn't right for them to having children before they're in a lasting relationship—that they must live with for the rest of their lives. Becca's confused and afraid for the future, but, like most people, she can't quite commit to self-inquiry and self-examination. She has real questions that need real answers, but she isn't willing to face the situation.

Feeling lost, she hears about sleep thinking from a friend and decides to try it out. She writes down a list of the things that seem to be troubling her. This is Becca's initial list:

)) Which major do I want, English or biology?
)) What job do I want in the future?
)) Why did I mess up that relationship with John?
)) What am I looking for in a guy?
)) Should I get a part-time job?
)) Do I want to go to graduate school?

As she looks over her list, she has the feeling that her questions have to do with an inability to commit, either to a major or to a relationship. Yet framing the matter as one of commitment doesn't feel quite right. She tries to get at what's really on her mind but suddenly loses patience and goes off to breakfast. In the face of her growing anxiety, she isn't able to pursue her desire to understand herself.

For her first night of sleep thinking, she decides to ask what seems like an innocent question: Which subject do I enjoy more, biology or English? As instructed, she tries to go to bed wondering rather than worrying about the answer. She knows that whatever choice she makes will affect her whole life, but still she tells herself to take it easy and just let an answer bubble up. But taking it easy turns out to be no easy matter! She thinks about her parents' desire for her to go to medical school, about how much college is costing, and about her friends' ideas about how life should be lived. Some of her friends say you need to choose a sensible profession; others say that the only "real" life is that of the writer. These thoughts weigh heavily on her as she gets ready for bed, and as a result, wondering and not worrying proves virtually impossible.

The first night, nothing happens during her sleep. She decides to try it again the next night and then the third night, but still nothing happens. She has no dreams and no thoughts whatsoever. In a corner of awareness, she knows that she's fighting with herself about whether or not she really wants an answer. On the fourth day, as she's walking across campus, she realizes that she is engaging in an internal debate. But she can't quite tell what's being debated. Then she hears herself saying, "No, I *do* want to know the truth!" Through some internal process, conducted for the most part out of conscious awareness, Becca has come around to wanting answers.

That night she knows exactly what question to sleep think: If I weren't afraid, which major would I choose? When she wakes up, she realizes that she's been thinking about all the microscopic entities she learned about last semester in her cell biology course. She wasn't dreaming; she was thinking about various cell parts, picturing and investigating them. She realizes that they actually interested her, not because her parents had medical school in mind for her and not because a career in biology would be more stable and lucrative than a career as a writer, but because they were fascinating in their own right. She isn't quite sure, but she has the feeling that she may be close to an answer.

All day she thinks about her thoughts from the previous night. Has she been fighting against biology just because her parents want her to study it? She goes over her feelings from the classes she's already taken in high school and college and has to admit that she's really enjoyed them. She likes biology. But does she like it enough to make it her life? For some reason, that question no longer makes her panic. She decides that she will sign up for the classes that are necessary for a biology major so that she can really prove to herself whether or not biology is the right path. She begins to feel excited about rather than afraid of the possibility that she's begun to plan for her future.

A few weeks later, after classes have started and she's feeling more comfortable academically, she decides to tackle the issue of her relationships. As happened the first time, with the question about majors, she sees that her first thought is, "I don't want to know." But now she can smile at her reluctance. She knows what question she wants to sleep think: What am I afraid of with respect to guys? What comes to her the very first night—again, not as a dream but as direct information—is the thought that dating and mating are two different things.

She suddenly realizes that her fear of commitment is just a smart, logical reaction to her situation. Given her many and varied opportunities to date and her need to find her life purpose, it would be a mistake to settle for an ordinary guy just because he had no serious faults. She can wait for love; she can wait for someone special; most importantly, she can take the time to become her own person. Suddenly she's no longer worried that she may meet Mr. Right and drop him because of some "fear of commitment." Her mantra becomes, "I can date; I can wait; I don't have to choose a life mate."

Brainstorm Current Issues and Questions

Your next task is to brainstorm issues and questions. That may sound as if I'm inviting you to do something pretty unchallenging. But that's not the case at all. What I'm asking you to do is to put all your cards on the table and to be honest with yourself about everything. For example, would it be easy to answer the following questions truthfully?

» What don't you like about yourself?
» What about your outlook needs changing?
» What behaviors need changing?
» What lies do you keep telling yourself?

Our first line of psychological defense is to lie to ourselves. But, usually this lying is not completely successful. Often we have an inkling of the truth somewhere in our awareness. For example, a man may say that his drinking isn't a problem, but in a corner of his mind, he knows that he really can't stop drinking once he starts. It may be that he doesn't want to stop; it may be that he's taking his revenge on the world by drinking and driving drunk. There may be all kinds of psychological and emotional reasons why he maintains his drinking behavior. But a glimmer of the truth is usually still available to him somewhere in consciousness.

It is those glimmers that you want to access. *Denial* is probably a slightly inaccurate word because it implies that the left hand and the right hand have no idea about each other. In the common view, a person in denial is entirely unaware of his or her own motives, which are hidden in a place called the unconscious. But I think that people know more about their own inner shenanigans than this view suggests.

I believe that you can access the truth if you are willing to. I hope that the first two steps of the sleep thinking program solidified your willingness so that now you feel ready to learn about your current problems and challenges. Your next goals are to access your truth and to generate a list of potential sleep thinking questions.

Following are seven ways to brainstorm a list of potential sleep thinking questions. Choose one that feels right for you. If your first attempt doesn't produce a substantial list of sleep thinking questions, use one of the other methods.

1. *Write your autobiography*. It should be at least 10 pages in length and as truthful and detailed as you can make it. Include your childhood experiences, what you were taught about life, how those lessons and experiences formed you, the consequences of any traumas (e.g., the death of a parent), and any unmet dreams (e.g., not getting a college degree). It should take you several days or even a week or more to write your autobiography. As you're writing it, jot down any questions that arise. Possibilities might include: Am I *still* grieving the loss of my mom, even after 20 years? Do I still feel abandoned? After you finish writing your autobiography, ask yourself, What issues are still challenging me? Turn each of these challenges into a question. For instance, if you sense that you have abandonment issues because of the early loss of a parent, ask questions such as: How are my abandonment issues still affecting me? or What can I do about my fear of abandonment?

2. *Visualize yourself being interviewed*. Imagine that you're both the interviewer and the subject of the interview. As interviewer, learn as much as you can about your subject before the

interview by looking at family photographs, chatting with rel-
atives (e.g., "Hi, mom, this is Mary. I'm going to interview
myself this evening and I need to know a little bit about myself
beforehand. So, who am I?"), reading old letters, and so on. Or
just think about yourself "from a distance," as if you were an
interviewer. Generate a list of questions for the interview,
questions as mundane as Where were you born? and as
pointed as You're very envious of your brother, aren't you? or
You've never worked very hard at anything, have you? Cull
from this long list of interview questions a shorter list that feels
as if it relates to your current situation.

   3. *Write a page or two in answer to the question, What are the
biggest challenges I'm facing right now?* When you've completed
the writing assignment, think about what you've written. You
may find that all of the challenges are connected by a single
theme (e.g., a lack of confidence or a sense of failure) or are
related to a single important change you need to make (e.g., a
career change or a relationship change). On the other hand, the
challenges may not seem to connect at all. In the first instance,
your list may be very short and sharply focused; in the second
instance, your list may be quite long and seemingly "all over
the map." Either way, reframe each challenge as a question, for
example, How can I gain some confidence? or What do I need
to do to rid myself of my sense of failure? Let your list be as
short or as long as necessary.

   4. *Look in the mirror and say Hi! What's bothering me these
days?* Wonder aloud about the things on your mind, about any
emotional or practical problems that are currently troubling
you. Try to smile at the image in the mirror; that way you'll get
a smile in return as you chat with yourself about your present
realities and your hopes for the future.

   5. *Consider the following list of skills or traits that researchers
feel are vital to the success of contemporary workers.*

Self-direction

Personal values

Thinking skills

Relationship skills

Confidence

Assertiveness

Energy

Awareness

Are you lacking in any of these skills? If you feel that you are, insert that skill into one of following questions: How can I improve my _____? or How can I become more _____? Generate as many of these questions as there are skills or traits you'd like to improve.

6. *Sleep think the question, What are my current issues?* Frame the question so that it resonates in your own ear. Here are some variations:

» What's bothering me?
» What do I need to do next?
» Where am I stuck?
» What's in my best interests to do?
» What should I focus on?

Choose one of these questions to sleep think. Tonight, once you're in bed, say it gently several times. Do not worry about getting answers. In fact, try not to worry about anything at all. You don't have to perform. You don't have to "try." You don't have to "think hard." Just say your question several times and fall asleep as usual.

Tomorrow morning take out your sleep thinking journal and prompt yourself with a little question such as, So? or Well? Relax and open up to your thoughts.

7. Just sit with a pad and pen or sit in front of your computer and brainstorm a list. It might be best to use a pad, because that gives you more freedom to jot down ideas "all over the place"—literally, all over the page. Such freedom is the essence of brainstorming. Once you've generated lots of thoughts about your current issues and problems, look them over, think about them, and pull them together into a single list.

Your goal is not to produce a long list or a short list of sleep thinking questions but to produce a truthful list, regardless of its length. You may have twenty questions on your list, or eight, or two. In a section of your sleep thinking journal that you devote to the lists you generate, write down your list of potential sleep thinking questions.

Identify Particular Issues and Questions to Focus On

Next, you'll want to choose a particular question to sleep think.

Denny, a forty-year-old computer analyst with several ill-defined worries about his current life, generated the following list of potential sleep thinking questions after he wrote, reread, and thought about his autobiography:

)) Why don't I want to spend more time with my wife and children, even though I know that I love them?

» Why am I so closed off?

» Why am I so stiff and formal? I know that people think I'm just a brain with no feelings at all. But that isn't true.

» I still can't figure out what I feel about my father. He was such a bastard, really. So, do I hate him? Or pity him? Or what?

» I'm already spending maybe 12 hours a day staring at a computer screen. Is this going to be my life for the next 20 or 25 years?

» I think I'm basically a very spiritual person, but I don't feel at all connected to . . . to what? Do I want a religion? What do I want?

» I'm still very sensitive about being a Mexican-American. I thought that by becoming a professional, my low self-esteem about the way I grew up and about Mexican-American stereotypes would disappear, but somehow they're more present than ever. What's up with that?

» I get very angry with my children sometimes—really rageful. Why is that? And over nothing!—why do I have such a short fuse?

» I keep coming back to those spiritual questions . . . and feeling so empty. Why do I feel so empty? I have so much, far more than I ever thought I'd have. So why do I feel all this emptiness?

When Denny reread his list he discovered that although all of the questions felt important, one stood out from the others. It was as if the question about his Mexican-American heritage chose him. It startled him that something that seemed so far in the past and that he thought he had put to rest felt so crucial to address. He also realized, though only vaguely, that the questions about his father, his rage, and his emptiness related to his childhood and his feelings about his culture. Although he had no idea that he'd be sleep thinking this particular question, once he generated his list and looked at the questions, he had no doubt about his choice.

When you read over your list you may not have the same strong, clear reaction that Denny had. You may be less certain about which question to choose. Don't worry. The goal of sleep thinking is not to choose the "perfect" question to sleep think. For several reasons, it isn't wise or sensible to put too high a premium on choosing the perfect question. First, the most relevant or important question may take some time to incubate. Second, it may only arrive after you've posed yourself some preliminary questions. Third, there may be no single question that needs answering but rather several equally important ones. So relax and don't worry or struggle when you read your list.

As you read your list, the most important or relevant question may pop right out at you, as it did for Denny. It may be one of those that you've been thinking about and struggling with for years. Or several questions may pop out at you, which together form a line of thought. For instance, when Mary, trying to figure out why she hated gallery openings so much, generated her list of sleep thinking questions, she realized several things: that she was harboring an unconscious hope that she'd be discovered at gallery openings, that in effect she was using gallery openings as her primary way of connecting with gallery owners and collectors, and that this meant that she was doing about as poor a job as she could of selling herself and her paintings.

Another possibility is that *all* of the questions on your list may seem relevant and important to you. Again, don't worry. All that means is that any question you choose will serve as an excellent starting point.

> $Q.$ *How do I know if I've chosen the right question to sleep think?*
>
> First, you need to be honest with yourself. In order to choose the best sleep thinking questions, you need to penetrate your defenses and arrive at a way of being that values and supports truthfulness.
>
> Second, you need to trust that you will be able to discern what you need to know. You need faith in yourself and in your ability to evaluate. Without this faith, you'll find yourself always turning toward others for answers. The best way to build trust in yourself is to consciously affirm that you are your own best expert.
>
> Third, you need to embrace both logic and intuition. Logic and intuition have to do with our talent for making important connections, sometimes in conscious awareness and sometimes not. To know whether a given question is the right one to sleep think, first think logically about the matter, asking questions of yourself such as, Is it logical that I should change jobs right now, given my circumstances? or Is it logical that I should write a novel all in verse, given that only one or two such novels ever get published?

But you also want to intuit whether you are on the right track and pay attention to any nagging doubts, little warning tingles, or to the chill that runs down your spine when you've hit on something right and important. It may not be logical to change jobs at this moment, but you may still know intuitively that it's the best thing to do. It may not be logical to write a verse novel, but you may know intuitively that you should do it anyway, even if it can't be published.

It isn't that intuition should be your only or even your primary guide, because sometimes you may discern that while it is intuitively right to do something—say, write that verse novel—there are still compelling logical reasons not to embark on that enterprise, and vice versa. The trick is to make sure that you keep both options open so that you can do the best job possible of sorting and connecting.

Look at the list you generated and take some time to choose a question from that list to sleep think. Don't worry whether you've chosen the very best question. Every good question gets a line of thought going, from which useful answers and more good questions flow.

So now you have your initial sleep thinking question. Let's get ready to take it to bed. ((·))

Getting Ready to Sleep Think

In this chapter, you'll learn how to negotiate steps 5 through 8 of the sleep thinking program (and begin sleep thinking the question you arrived at in the last chapter):

Step 5. Manage anxiety.

Step 6. Refashion bedtime so that you're prepared to sleep think.

Step 7. Fall asleep with a wonder, not a worry.

Step 8. Surrender to nighttime brain work.

Manage Anxiety

Fear and anxiety are necessary to our survival; they are our warning system. Because we have no way of knowing for certain which events are safe and which are dangerous, our early warning system alerts us—and bedevils us—a great deal of the time. We are overwarned; rather than err on the side of under-protecting us, our early warning system alerts us at the merest hint of danger.

Sometimes our warning signals are entirely appropriate. Imagine feeling hungry and desperate and coming upon a wild mushroom, or driving, against your better judgment, through a fog bank. Your body wells up with anxiety, rightly warning you that what you are about to do or what is about to happen may be dangerous. There are countless situations in which it is imperative that we have this warning system, for example, when we want to change a light fixture but haven't turned off the electricity, when a tornado appears in the distance, when a barroom brawl breaks out at the next table. Without such a good warning system, we'd be too vulnerable to survive as a species. But our mind and body can overdo it. For example, germs do cause disease, but demanding that people wash their hands with the antiseptic soap you carry around with you before they can play with your baby is going too far and signals that you are full of anxiety. Some spiders are poisonous, but having an enormous whole body alert reaction at the sight of a household spider is too big a reaction to the circumstances and speaks to the mind's ability to see danger where there isn't much of any.

Worse and most disabling is that we can have vague but powerful fears and anxieties about *everything*. This free-floating anxiety latches on to the next thing in view. Once we've convinced ourselves that the door is really locked and we can go on to work, then we worry about whether the bus will be late and that by being late we'll get in trouble at the office. Then, when the bus arrives on time, we begin to worry about the tasks piled up our desk. When, by the end of the day, we've reduced that pile to next to nothing, we worry about how bad traffic will be getting home and whether our stocks have taken a hit while we weren't watching them.

It is no longer fashionable to talk about an "age of anxiety," as it was in the 1950s and 1960s, yet we are definitely still living in one. Now we tend to call it "stress." Because of this stress or anxiety, millions of Americans—some estimate the number as high as 80 million—are insomniacs. Stress can keep people awake or infiltrate their sleep. If you're so stressed out that you're still worrying about things once you fall asleep, how much good sleep thinking can go on? It's much more likely that you'll have anxiety dreams, nightmares, or just a restless, tossing-and-turning few hours in bed rather than a productive sleep thinking experience.

A goal of the sleep thinking program is to reduce the stress and anxiety in your life so that you can effectively sleep think. This is an ambitious goal. But any step you take in the direction of reducing your stress, however small, increases your ability to calmly pose your sleep thinking question and engage your brain while you sleep. So take a little time now and read over the suggested anxiety management strategies. I hope you'll decide to pick a strategy (or two) and begin to incorporate it into your life. Remember: It is very hard to sleep think if you are stressed and anxious, so getting calmer is not just a generally good idea but really crucial to making the sleep thinking program work.

Following are six anxiety-management strategies. Look them over, then choose one or two to practice and learn.

1. Relaxation techniques. There are many different relaxation techniques available to you, including progressive relaxation exercises, self-massage, self-hypnosis, the Sarnoff Squeeze, the Quieting Reflex, and so on. Renee Harmon presents a short progressive relaxation exercise in her book *How to Audition for Movies and TV*. Her exercise only takes about 30 seconds:

》 Consciously relax your forehead.

》 Consciously relax the areas around your eyes.

》 Consciously relax the corners of your mouth.

》 Listen to the sounds around you but do not concentrate on them.

》 Feel your arms and legs become heavy. At the point of the most intense heaviness, imagine that all your tension flows out of your body. Your fingertips are the exit points.

》 Feel sunshine warm your stomach.

》 Lift your chin and smile.

2. Breathing techniques. In his book *Managing Your Anxiety*, Christopher McCullough describes several simple breathing techniques. The exercises have names like "slow, complete breathing," "slow, deep breathing with shoulder relaxation," "counting breaths," "following your breathing," and "circling your breaths." "Circling your breaths," for example, works as follows:

As you start to inhale, you slowly bring your attention up the ventral centerline of your body from the groin to the navel, chest, throat, and face, until you reach the crown of your head. As you exhale, slowly move your attention down the back of the head, down the neck, and all the way down the spine.

Stephanie Judy has a simple breathing exercise in her book *Making Music for the Joy of It:*

Anxiety disrupts normal breathing patterns, producing either shallow breathing or air gulping in an attempt to conserve the body's supply of oxygen. The simplest immediate control measure is to exhale, blowing slowly and steadily through your lips until your lungs feel completely empty. Don't "breathe deeply." It's too easy to hyperventilate and make yourself dizzy. As long as you make a slow, full exhale, the inhaling will look after itself.

3. Guided Visualizations. Guided visualizations are mental pictures you create for yourself. For instance, imagine yourself in a tranquil spot—at the beach, in a garden, beside a secluded lake—and spend time there, in your mind's eye, relaxing and letting your worries slip away. The pianist Andrea Bodo, for example, created, as part of her five-step routine to help her calmly make her entrance onstage, a guided visualization in which she transported herself to a spot beside a pool filled with water lilies.

Use your guided visualization in the following way:

» First, seat yourself comfortably, placing your feet squarely on the ground.
» Then, shut your eyes.
» Next, start with a progressive relaxation or breathing exercise to calm yourself so that you drift into the sort of receptive state in which images flow.
» Then, either silently or out loud, give yourself cues to produce the desired images in your mind. A typical string of cues might sound like the following: "I'm driving to the lake. I'm almost there now. I think I'll be able to see it when I get around the next bend. Yes, there it is!"
» Finally, stay "in" the place you've created until you can feel your tensions easing.

4. Discharge techniques. It's possible to reduce stress and alleviate anxiety by discharging your pent-up worries through exercise, physical activity, or physical gestures such as primal screams, shadow boxing, pillow beating, or battle cries. Each of these can be done in dramatic fashion or in a more subdued way; for example, you can actually scream, which might scare the neighbors and bring the police, or you can achieve stress relief with a silent scream. You can also discharge pent-up stress by laughing, by making zany faces, through sexual relations, or simply by moving about.

A little exercise can help a lot. You can jog in place, skip rope, or dance in your nightclothes. One study found that subjects who engaged in aerobics upped their NREM sleep, the period during which prime sleep thinking occurs, by a full third. Others study have shown that people who exercise take less time to fall asleep and sleep significantly longer.

5. *Cognitive Work.* One important way to reduce stress and anxiety is to change the way you think about things. One person may be stressed out waiting in a slow-moving line and another person can remain relaxed because he or she isn't making the situation worse by saying things to himself or herself such as "Won't this damned line ever move?" or "That clerk is doing as much talking as checking!" What you say to yourself in a given situation and about that situation are the greatest determinants of whether or not you will feel stress in that situation.

We tend to speak to ourselves in negative, inaccurate, and distorting ways. This inner language contributes to our experience of stress. Cognitive therapists have developed many strategies for managing our inner talk, strategies with names such as decentering, thought stopping, thought substitution, stress inoculation, cognitive modeling, and decatastrophizing. All of these techniques can be used to identify and change this inner language, which is often all it takes to reduce or eliminate our stress.

6. *Dietary and Lifestyle Changes.* A holistic approach to stress management includes consideration of all aspects of

your life. Is your alcohol consumption increasing your stress and your insomnia? Are you ingesting caffeine so late in the day that your evenings are edgy and your sleep jagged? Is your diet helping or harming you? Are you lacking some essential ingredients in your diet? Are there some herbal remedies that might calm you? Are you burning the candles at both ends or living such a stressful life that simple stress management techniques may not help enough?

Pick one or two of the strategies and learn about them. This may mean getting a book on breathing techniques, finding out whether your health care provider sponsors biofeedback workshops, spending a few sessions with a therapist who specializes in cognitive therapy, visiting your local herbalist, or taking the time to design a guided visualization and then using it on a regular basis.

Part of your bedtime ritual, which I'll discuss next, should include the anxiety management strategy you've chosen. So I hope you'll actually have chosen one and practiced it a little before you proceed to the next step.

$Q.$ *I still think that my anxiety will get in the way of my sleep thinking. What should I do?*

Become an anxiety intuitive. Anxiety intuitives are people who are smart and knowledgeable about their own anxieties and know how to get rid of them or, when necessary, just embrace them. Sometimes we get anxious. That's normal, natural, and inevitable. But several other things are also true: that we often get *too* anxious, that we contribute to our anxiety by the way we talk to ourselves and by the way we view situations, and, on a positive note, that we're able to reduce and even eliminate a lot of anxiety from our life by becoming more aware of the many ways we magnify risks.

Many therapists believe that you need to know where your anxiety comes from in order to treat it. I don't agree. I think you just need to see it more clearly and really acknowledge its existence. If you deny its existence, it does its damage anyway, and you have no chance of getting rid of it. But if you can learn that anxiety is a warning signal of danger and a very inaccurate one, like a smoke alarm that goes off whenever you light a candle, and if you can train yourself to look behind the anxiety to see whether any real danger exists, you will find that your experience of anxiety diminishes greatly.

An anxiety intuitive knows that the mind makes anxiety and that the mind makes big mistakes. It can translate little threats or nonthreats into big threats. The mind scares the body. So anxiety isn't the problem. The problem is that we are so good at making ourselves anxious. When you become an anxiety intuitive, you become an expert at seeing that *virtually all of the time*, no real threat is present.

Refashion Bedtime So That You're Prepared to Sleep Think

What do people do in the last hour before they fall asleep? They watch television. They read a book. They make love. A few meditate. Some drink or use street drugs or prescription drugs. Some brood about what tomorrow will bring or rehash the day's events in their mind. Some are still working right up to the last minute, either doing chores that didn't get done during the day or work related to their job. Virtually no one is spending any time getting ready to use sleep as a time for thinking.

Consider Molly. Molly was pretty typical of today's insomniac. At 28, she worked at a stressful job as a property manager, managing a complex of two hundred townhouse apartments, and was also raising a daughter by herself. Adopted as an infant, she had the additional stress of having her birth mother enter the picture just the previous year. In addition, her adoptive mother was dying from cancer. Every night Molly spent time getting her 5-year-old to bed, then watched television in the hopes that she would get drowsy and fall asleep. But usually she couldn't fall asleep until the wee hours of the morning and then usually slept no more than 3 or 4 hours.

What seemed to be keeping her up were thoughts about her birth mother, who turned out to be a needy, critical person who continually asked Molly to forgive her for giving her up for adoption but who also incessantly criticized Molly about the way she was raising her daughter. She didn't like the name Molly had given her daughter—Gerry—which she found too masculine. In addition, she didn't like the way Molly dressed Gerry, or the food Molly fed her. Cynthia, Molly's mom, had moved all the way from Detroit to San Francisco to be near Molly, so as to "make up" for giving her away, and now she seemed to be forever calling or coming over.

It was clear to Molly what question she wanted to sleep think: What can I do about Cynthia? But she found it impossible to focus on the question in a productive way. She found herself exhausted at night but also too agitated and restless to even frame the question to herself, let alone frame it in a calm, meditative way. So Molly and I discussed how she might reorganize bedtime in order to give herself a better chance of sleeping and sleep thinking. Together we created the following bedtime ritual:

1. Molly would set herself a bedtime. She chose 11:30 P.M.

2. At 8, she would read Gerry a story. Then she would tuck Gerry in, tell her she loved her, and shut Gerry's door.

3. She would make herself an herb tea and watch television until 11. Usually this meant that she would watch two hour-long shows, one starting at 9 and one at 10.

4. At eleven she would turn off the television, get out of bed—where she'd been watching her shows—and sit on a pillow on the floor in a position she'd learned in a yoga class. Getting in this position helped Molly think of what she was doing as special and ceremonial. She would begin by doing a breathing exercise she liked, which was really a small meditation exercise as well, in which she would count her breaths on the inhale, counting to five, and then say to herself "don't know" on the exhale.

5. The last thing she would do, after brushing her teeth and getting ready for bed, would be to tell herself a certain joke that always made her laugh, so that she could crawl into bed in a light mood.

6. In bed, she wouldn't think about her mother at all, because thinking about her only meant getting angry and upset about the whole situation. So she "thought blocked" Cynthia, which meant that she needed to have ready a "thought substitute." When Cynthia came to mind, she pictured Gerry instead.

7. Then she would begin to count slowly in the dark, her eyes closed, and when she started to feel drowsy, she would make the conscious effort to smile inwardly and say to herself, "What should I do about Cynthia?"

This ritual worked well for Molly. In just a few days, it came to her that she had to do a very dramatic, difficult, and painful thing, but one that felt absolutely right. She had to tell Cynthia that she didn't want her in her life, at least not at this time. Her adoptive mother needed her and so did her daughter, and she had no room in her life for Cynthia. In fact, her decision led to a fight and a rupture, but still Molly felt certain that she was doing the right thing.

Just in case she wasn't doing the right thing, she formulated another sleep thinking question: Is there any way to have a decent relationship with Cynthia? Employing the same bedtime ritual, which she now used all the time because it had cured her insomnia, she posed that new question. The answer came to her in several different ways, but in each case, the answer was the same: For her own sake and for that of her daughter, she had to avoid her birth mother.

In your sleep thinking journal, write down your thoughts about the kind of bedtime ritual that might work for you. Read over Molly's ritual and consider the sorts of things she included. Try to picture each step of your new ritual and try to identify and articulate what you're trying to accomplish with each step.

Your bedtime ritual may involve many steps or it may involve only a few. There's no right or wrong here. But you may have to try out your ritual several times before you come up with one that works just right.

Fall Asleep with a Wonder, Not a Worry

The most important part of your new bedtime ritual is the very last part. In bed, as you're getting ready to fall asleep, you say your question, to yourself or out loud, in a gentle, meditative way.

You may be thinking, "Why should I go to bed interrogating myself?" The answer has three parts. First, most people already go to bed worried about something; it may be worry over an unpleasant task at work, outstanding bills, or their child's school problems. They brood about these problems as they try to fall asleep. What happens then? They take a long time falling asleep, and they don't sleep very well. Nor do they get their problems solved that way. If most adults went to bed without a care in the world and then slept like a baby, it would certainly be wise to wonder whether asking themselves provocative questions at bedtime made sense. But good, restful sleep is a blessing that already eludes a great many Americans. So they have nothing to lose.

Second, while a percentage of the millions of people suffering from insomnia have some physical disease or physiological change such as menopause contributing to sleeplessness, an even larger number, the lion's share, are kept awake by feelings of pessimism and hopelessness. People get stuck believing that their problems are unsolvable and give up on the possibility of finding answers. This vicious cycle, in which people worry but don't feel that they can solve their problems—which makes them worry more—makes people pessimistic and despondent. A lot of our current depression epidemic is rooted in this pessimism.

An air of defeat begins to hang over people trapped this way. They don't know what kind of work to pursue. Though they have many ways to communicate available to them—they can send faxes, e-mails, and so on—they feel isolated and estranged. They can learn the latest news in an instant, yet they have the feeling that they know less and less about what's really going on. All of this leads to agitation and despair.

I've engaged in what may seem like a digression to make a little more clear why there is really no risk in sleep thinking. Most people are already worried, and these worries are not of the sort that go away easily, because of our uncertainties about how life ought to be lived. This leads to the third reason why you might as well go to bed with a question in mind: Sleep thinking can do far more than help you solve this or that problem. It can help you make the shift from pessimism to optimism, from hopelessness to hope, from meaninglessness to new meanings. The underlying feeling-tones of sleep thinking are hope, optimism, and affirmation, and it is these feelings that you communicate to yourself by the very way you pose your question.

That's the primary difference between "a wonder" and "a worry." It has to do with the underlying hopefulness that lightens a wonder and not just with the words you choose to use. If you go to bed saying to yourself, "I hate my supervisor, and I don't see how I can survive her criticisms another day," you'll toss and turn and probably find yourself wandering around the house at 2 A.M. But if you say to yourself, "I wonder if there are some skills I can learn to survive a toxic boss?" and if you couple that wonder with an inner smile and some real lightness, believing that answers are available to you, then you'll fall asleep quickly and sleep think answers.

You want to bring feelings of optimism and hopefulness to your self-questioning. You also want to choose your language carefully so that it supports an open-ended, wondering way of being, rather than a closed-down, all-is-lost one. Sometimes all that's needed is to add the phrase *I wonder* to the basic question and making some minimal other changes, as in the following examples:

)) Worry: "I can't get out of debt."
Wonder: "I wonder how I can get out of debt."

)) Worry: "I'm in a dead-end job."
Wonder: "I wonder how I can get out of my dead-end job."

)) Worry: "I'll never stick to this diet."
Wonder: "I wonder how I can stick to this diet."

))   Worry: "It's impossible to get Jack to have a real conversation with me."
Wonder: "I wonder if it's possible to get Jack to have a
real conversation with me."

Sometimes it's necessary to do some extra reframing,
especially when a word in the question is so charged that it
will be hard for you to think clearly about the issues involved.
In the following examples, *cheating, loser, coward*, and *hate* are
such words and need to be excised:

))   Worry: "Is Lilith cheating on me?"
Wonder: "I wonder what's going on between Lilith and
me that feels so weird and unpleasant."

))   Worry: "Why am I such a loser?"
Wonder: "I wonder why I'm having so much trouble following through on my dreams."

))   Worry: "Why am I a complete coward?"
Wonder: "I wonder why taking risks feels so scary
to me."

))   Worry: "I know that Dad hates me now because of the
abortion. What can I do?"
Wonder: "I wonder what can be done about the rift
between me and Dad?"

Now that you have a better idea of the difference between
a wonder and a worry, go back to your sleep thinking question
and see whether it feels correctly framed. Play with it until it
does. Then write it down in big letters on a clean sheet of paper

or give it a whole page in your sleep thinking journal. Your sleep thinking question is ready.

> Q. *I don't really like the idea of losing sleep and being bothered with recording things in the middle of the night. Besides, can't I become sleep deprived if my brain gets too active and keeps waking me up every night?*
>
> Let's take the second part of the question first. People who are deprived of a lot of sleep—people trying to stay awake for some reason, say, because they are trying to break a record—usually recover quickly and completely after 12 to 14 hours of sleep.
>
> The researcher James Horne, in his book *Why We Sleep*, makes an interesting distinction between what he calls "core sleep" and "optional sleep." From his experimental research and understanding of the sleep literature, he concludes that the first 4 or 5 hours of sleep are really needed, and the rest of the sleep cycle, including the lion's share of REM sleep, is not really needed. So if, say, you go to bed at 11 and are awakened at 3 (during NREM sleep, while you're thinking) with a thought, in an important sense, you've slept enough already and shouldn't be harmed at all, even if you were to stay up the rest of the night.
>
> As to not liking to be awakened, that's natural. Typically, we enjoy our sleep, and for lots of us, getting to sleep and staying there are so difficult that the thought of interrupting our precious sleep seems like a bad idea. But keep in mind that you are inter-

rupting your sleep for the sake of your own ideas, you will probably be awakened only very occasionally, and you will be up for so short a time that going back to sleep shouldn't prove too difficult. I think you'll see that even though you don't like the idea of getting up in the middle of night, on balance it's a useful thing to get accustomed to doing. And probably, it will happen only rarely!

Surrender to Nighttime Brain Work

Even if you accomplish steps 1 through 7, there's still a switch you have to throw in order to sleep think. If you don't, you won't sleep think to your full potential or possibly even sleep think much at all. The switch you have to throw is the one that relinquishes your conscious control of the process and allows you to surrender to whatever your night mind wants to deliver up to you.

Surrendering to your nighttime brain work means letting down your guard and permitting your mind to do whatever work it needs to do, including straining to make connections, visiting dark, secretive places, and other hard or dangerous things. If you don't like to do these things while you're awake, you won't want to do them when you're asleep either. If, for instance, you're afraid to create during the day and never started writing that mystery novel you always said you wanted to write, you won't be inclined to start it while you sleep. So surrendering to this night work also means surrendering in a round-the-clock way to the many risks inherent in living an aware, creative, and fulfilled life.

Surrendering is a quiet acknowledgment and acceptance of risk. Take Irene, for example. Irene had always wanted to write. She'd also wanted to get an advanced degree in anthropology and do research. But she seemed to fall short on all of her dreams. Not only didn't she get an advanced degree, she never got her undergraduate degree. And not only didn't she write, but she found it painfully hard to write even the simplest things, like thank-you notes and business e-mail.

She called herself blocked and likened what she was experiencing to having a black cloud over her head all the time. She felt strongly that her childhood experiences had a tremendous amount to do with her adult problems, but she'd never really stopped to think in what ways those childhood traumas had impaired her or what she might do to help herself overcome them. She tried to stay on top of things by exerting control—over her body by exercising strenuously, even when injured, and by eating very little, even to the point of starvation. Not only did she never surrender, but she hated the word.

Finally, she saw that she wasn't making it in life. Not only did her marriage fall apart, not only did she self-destruct at work, but she even had a break with reality. In therapy, after the acute but short-lasting break, she began to understand that she couldn't control life. She could only meet it, think about it, make certain changes and not others, and surrender to reality. She could only accomplish what she could accomplish, which, to begin with, was taking one junior college course.

Because she was starting to know her own nature, she knew that she had to be careful not to make a grandiose leap to the belief that getting her doctoral degree was just around the corner. She had to continue surrendering to the truth, which had its negative as well as its positive aspects. On the negative side, it wasn't possible to accomplish everything in a day, and in fact, it was going to take her many years, a lot of sweat, and some real setbacks before she could fulfill her dreams. On the positive side, she began to feel less pressure to control everything and less reason to consider herself a failure.

She had to do the same sort of surrendering when it came to sleep thinking. She had to accept that answers wouldn't come on demand, that sometimes they wouldn't come at all, that sometimes they'd come but she'd have trouble understanding or interpreting them—that, in short, she couldn't control the process or guarantee her success with it. All she could do was faithfully try. To do otherwise would be to engage in the kind of magical thinking—oh, I can get a Ph.D. just like that!—that had prevented her from achieving her goals. She began to see that surrender was both a reality check and an opening to her better, more hopeful, and more optimistic nature.

I hope you'll find the willingness to surrender to the night. Let your brain deliver up whatever it wishes. Be brave about sleep thinking and frame it as an act of courage as well as a way of solving problems. Many people, even the most intelligent and sensitive, never find the wherewithal to do this surrendering and, therefore, do not make much use of the night. I hope you find that wherewithal and flip the switch that permits your brain to engage itself.

Sleep Thinking Pledge

I am willing to sleep think. This means that I relinquish control over my mind at night, I surrender to whatever work it wants to do, and I pledge my willingness to look at and think about whatever it wants to present me with, whenever sleep thoughts decide to make themselves known, whether during the middle of the night, or early in the morning. Furthermore, I agree to start every day prepared to receive whatever my mind wants to deliver from the night. I will pose to myself a sleep thinking question every night, as a prompt, and I will change my sleep thinking question as circumstances dictate. I accept that my sleep thoughts may suggest that I have work to do, and I will do that work. In all of this, I surrender to the power available in my own brain and to my own enormous capacity to think while I sleep.

You are now ready to begin sleep thinking. With the first eight steps under your belt, you now have a particular question to sleep think, a new bedtime ritual, and a sense of how to surrender to the night.

If you've been reading along and not doing the exercises, I invite you to stop and catch up. Spend a little time working the first eight steps. Then choose a night to begin your sleep thinking.

You may learn something important the first night. You may begin to change the first night. Or, like every sleep thinker, you may have a mixed bag of experiences, fruitless nights followed by a night of revelation, or nights of confusion followed by one instant of clarity.

What will your experience be like? The only way to find out is to begin. ((·))

Evaluating Sleep Thoughts

In this chapter we examine steps 9 through 11 of the sleep thinking program:

Step 9. Arise during the night to record your thoughts, if your thoughts awaken you.

Step 10. Spend time first thing each morning processing the night.

Step 11. Make sense of the information you receive.

A large part of your success with the sleep thinking program will depend upon whether you accept your own sleep thoughts as valuable. This means getting up in the middle of the night if a sleep thought or important dream awakens you and recording it; spending time each morning, whether or not a thought or dream feels present, to give yourself time for sleep thoughts to come forward; and making the effort to interpret and evaluate your sleep thoughts.

Arise During the Night to Record Your Thoughts, If Your Thoughts Awaken You

Do you remember the anecdote I related earlier about the German physiologist Otto Loewi? It took him 17 years to sleep think the experiment that would prove his theory about the chemical transmission of nerve impulses, and when it came to him in the middle of the night, he woke up and scribbled down his thoughts. But in the morning, he couldn't read his own writing! Nor could he remember what his idea had been. Fortunately for him, at three o'clock the next morning, the idea returned. This time he didn't write his idea down; instead, he went directly to the laboratory and conducted the experiment that had come to him in his sleep.

Loewi was lucky that the idea for his experiment returned the second night. While such luck makes sense in his case, because of his years of preparation, there is no guarantee that the fruits of sleep thinking will always come back a second time. That's why it's vital for sleep thinkers awakened in the middle of the night by a meaningful dream or idea to carefully record the fruits of their sleep thinking. They may even want to do more than record their idea; they may want to work on it, elaborate it, or understand it right then and there, in the dead of the night, as Loewi did.

Most people don't like to do this. We've all had the experience of waking up in the middle of the night with a solution to a problem or with an idea that feels important enough to be revisited in the morning. But most of us feel a little threatened by this experience, even though it's just our brain working freely and well. Something about the experience disturbs us and even scares us. We're a little unnerved by our own solutions and by the feeling of excitement, even of awe, that accompany such moments. We have the inclination to dampen our own enthusiasm and quietly forget what our brain just dreamed up.

It is important to change how you feel about being awakened by your thoughts, to move from disliking such events to anticipating them with relish. To accomplish this, follow these suggestions:

1. *Have a pad by your bed, so that you can write down the thoughts that awaken you.* Keep an ordinary notepad by your bed, rather than your journal. You can record your night thoughts using that pad, then transfer what you've written to your sleep thinking journal in the morning. This way you can use the act of transferring what you've written as an opportunity to elaborate on your thoughts and make additional connections.

2. *Have some good ideas about what you'll do if you become so wide awake during the night that you can't fall right back asleep.* This is important. You don't want your fear of ruining your night's sleep to stop your brain from thinking. You might keep a good book handy and read a few pages of it after you've recorded your sleep thoughts. You might calmly make yourself a cup of tea, telling yourself that it isn't urgent that you fall right back asleep, or you might do a few minutes of exercise or a little yoga. What's important is that you feel prepared, so that your brain can relax and do its best thinking.

3. *Resume sleeping with a new wonder based on what you've just uncovered.* The thought that awakened you may seem

only modestly interesting, or it may seem extremely interesting. If it is extremely interesting, you may have to fully awaken and begin processing it right then and there, writing about it, interpreting it, and making sense of it. If it is only moderately interesting, you can probably go right back to sleep, either directly or after you've read a few pages of your bedside book. In either case, once you go back to bed and are getting ready to fall asleep again, let yourself wonder about what you've learned. Use the rest of the night as an opportunity to further sleep think.

4. *Learn to love rather than dread the excitement of being awakened in the middle of the night by your own thoughts.* Say things to yourself such as, "I can hardly wait to see what my brain wants to send me tonight!" Feel eager rather than doubtful, curious rather than worried. Adopt the attitude that you are positively looking forward to being awakened.

Jack was a good example of someone who started the sleep thinking program with high hopes. He had every intention of solving the problem he had with his elderly mother, who needed assistance with her needs but was adamantly refusing Jack's help. Jack got his question framed and started sleep thinking, but when thoughts struck him in the middle of the night several nights in a row, instead of getting up and recording them, he turned over and went back to sleep. Each morning, even though he sat at his desk and tried to remember, he couldn't bring those thoughts back. Within a week, his reluctance to wake up and record his thoughts and his sense that the answers he needed had permanently eluded him sapped his motivational strength and made him want to stop the program.

I suggested to Jack that he might have a problem with the middle of the night; something about coming fully awake might be bothering him deeply. Rather than trying to identify the problem, I wondered whether it might be a better idea to just try to get more comfortable with waking up in the middle of the night, for example, by doing something—anything— and then going back to sleep. In that way, he would see that there was no threat involved and nothing to fear, that he could tolerate being up at that time of night and that he could suc- cessfully return to sleep after awakening.

We mapped out some things for him to do in the fol- lowing week. First, he'd use his alarm clock to get him up at 3 A.M. each night. (It's good to set up exercises of this sort so as not to interfere with the first four hours of sleep, which are your core hours of sleep. Loss of sleep during these hours is less desirable than loss of sleep later on during the night. Since Jack typically went to bed at about 11, I chose 3 A.M. as the time for him to arise.) The first night he was to wake up, make himself a bowl of instant onion soup, consume it, and then go back to bed. The second night he was to wake up, study a little Greek, which he harbored the dream of learning, and then go back to bed. Jack and I created similar tasks for the whole week.

When I saw Jack next he reported that the first night he hadn't been able to stay up at all and that the second night netted him the same results. The third night he'd sat up, thought about making himself a cup of soup, but decided against it and went back to sleep. The fourth night, though, he awoke not because his alarm went off but because a thought struck him, and this time he turned on the light, woke completely up, and wrote his thought down. Although he was afraid that he'd have trouble getting back to sleep, in fact, once he hopped back into bed, he fell asleep almost instantly. He thought that he might as well discontinue the experiment because that one night taught him the lesson he needed to learn: that it was going to be okay to completely awaken when sleep thoughts came to him. He concluded that for whatever reasons, he was no longer afraid of the night.

Spend Time First Thing Each Morning Processing the Night

Some people wake up and spend time with their yoga, meditation practice, or journal writing. But the vast majority of people launch right into their workday rituals of showering, dressing, getting the kids off to school, and getting themselves off to work. Breakfast is cold cereal or a waffle popped into the toaster, a second cup of coffee is a luxury, and everyone in the house feels rushed and anxious. The day's worries are already present, and nothing about the night and its messages can be considered or processed.

Sleep thinkers change their relationship to morning. Even if they have to get right off to work or get the kids up and out the door, they still learn to set aside some time each morning, right after they awaken, to process what their sleep thinking has uncovered. This becomes like a meditation or religious practice, something separate from their usual activities and even a little sacred. In order to do this, most sleep thinkers have to get up a little earlier than they previously did, maybe even a whole hour earlier. Though they may resist at first, once they understand the potential rewards and actually start to be rewarded, they manage to get up earlier.

Here are the steps for beginning your day as a sleep thinker:

1. Work the program. If you aren't actively wrestling with a problem, issue, or creative project, if you haven't gotten into the habit of enlisting your brain at night, you won't feel very motivated to get up early. In fact, your brain will have that much less information to provide you with, and you may not find your morning work very productive.

2. Practice getting up early enough so that you have time for your sleep thought processing. If you now get up at 6:30 and have no extra time for anything but getting ready for work, you will need to get up at 5:30. If you lead a leisurely life, a retired life, or one in which you set your own schedule, then there is no need to get up any earlier than usual. But if the time right after you awaken is already completely taken up with your prework routine, you will need to practice getting up an hour earlier each morning. This requires a mind and body shift and isn't easy to accomplish. If you're very motivated and very lucky, you may accomplish this shift in a matter of days or weeks. If you're more typical, it may take you months. However long it takes, it is essential that you acquire this extra time.

3. Whatever time you get up, whether earlier than before because you need the extra hour or at your usual time because your schedule is your own, you have the task of actually getting to your desk first thing. Of course, you can brush your teeth and pour yourself a cup of coffee. In our household, I have to spend a few seconds feeding the

cats or all hell would break loose. But there isn't much more that you should permit yourself to do before you start processing. You don't want to check your e-mail, do a little yoga and stretching, or anything of that sort. Get to your desk as quickly as you can.

4. Consciously acknowledge that the pressures of the day are already weighing on you (if that's the case) and that it's hard to sit quietly with your own thoughts when there are tasks to do and worries on your mind. It's not easy to be calm in such circumstances, and this is why so many would-be creative people, who dream of getting up and doing their creative work first thing each morning, usually decide to put off their efforts until evening, when, usually, they find themselves too tired to begin. Morning is the ideal time for processing your sleep thoughts, so it's important that you understand just how hard it may be to sit calmly at your desk with the pressure of the day already on your shoulders. The only answer is to talk yourself into the belief that this hour is sacred, that you need it and deserve it, and that there's really no danger in putting off the start of your "real" day for an hour.

5. Learn for yourself how to run with your own ideas first thing each morning. I like to work at a computer. You may find that you like to use a yellow legal pad or a journal. I don't use any particular prompt to help me process the night. I just sit and begin writing, most often on my current book but sometimes on particular issues and problems I'm working on. Indeed, the simplest and most straightforward way to begin each morning is just to pick up the train of thought on your current issue, not concerning yourself with your night thoughts but just pre-

suming—rightly—that whatever you are now thinking has been informed by the night. However, you may want to use a prompt to help you begin, or you may want to consciously adopt a certain attitude. For example, you might do the following:

» Repeat your sleep thinking question and ask yourself, "What am I learning?"
» See what you last recorded in your journal on your current issue and then quietly say, "What's new?"
» Free write a little, beginning with, "I'm thinking about . . ." or, "What's on my mind is . . ."
» Just sit, unworried and unruffled, and quietly say a Zen phrase such as *no mind* or *nothing*.
» Sit with an attitude of eagerness and curiosity, wondering to yourself what excellent solutions to your current problems your brain may have landed upon during the night.

I've spent time talking about how to start the day as a creative person in two of my previous books, *Fearless Creating* and *The Creativity Book*, and you might want to peek at them for a further discussion of how to begin each morning in right self-relationship.

Your goals for the hour you spend each morning processing the night are four-fold: to allow sleep thoughts to come forward, to not let your mind drift off to affairs of the day, to interpret the thoughts that arrive, and to prepare yourself for the work that your sleep thoughts suggest. That's a lot. But all of that is within your grasp and, once you become practiced at processing the night, easy to attain.

Make Sense of the Information You Receive

This step is sometimes the hardest step and sometimes the easiest step of the sleep thinking program. Often it can be the easiest. However the information from your sleep thinking efforts arrives—in a dream, as an image, as an intuition, or as a direct thought—if it's clear, unequivocal, and feels right, then there's nothing simpler than making sense of what you've received. It's a done deal, so to speak. There's no interpreting to do. When the therapist I quoted in the first chapter realized in her sleep how to solve her algebra problem, there was nothing else for her to do. Her sleep thought was the equivalent of a clear, complete solution.

Often you have little or no doubt that what you've received from your sleep thinking is the answer you've been awaiting. It just has that intuitive feeling of rightness to it. You wake up knowing that you're supposed to make a certain phone call, say something to a particular person, start the home business you've been dreaming of beginning, or launch a new book or painting. Of course, the actual work still has to be done—making the phone call, starting the business, painting the picture—but the information is clear, the moment is ripe, and there is nothing at all to interpret.

But this clarity doesn't come all of the time or even most of the time. How could it? The things on our mind are complicated, hard to unravel, slippery, even downright contradictory. More importantly, gaining self-awareness and arriving at self-information are more like processes than events. Your brain makes connections, rejects and accepts ideas, changes its mind, and so forth. What you receive in a sleep thought is likely to be a marker in that process and not the finished product, which hasn't yet had the time to emerge.

So you'll need a method of making sense of information that is obscurely presented, hard to seize hold of, hard to make heads or tails of, too fragmentary, or a confusing marker in a complicated, ongoing process. The best way of dealing with uncertain information is to relax and to sleep think on it again. Just say "Hmm," lightly consider what the dream, image, intuition, or thought might mean, avoid straining or forcing an interpretation, and remark to yourself, "Looks like I have something new to sleep think!"

You can't force an interpretation on a dream or a thought, though you can certainly mull the dream or thought over and wonder what it's about. You can certainly say, "Given what I know about myself, what does this dream suggest?" You can certainly say, "I seem to be thinking that I should be calling my father, but is that what I really mean?" You can and should communicate with yourself about your own thoughts and feelings. But you can't force a dream or a thought to give up its secrets—if there are any secrets there to be given up—nor can you go to a dream cookbook and use some recipe to help with the interpreting.

Take Mark. A computer engineer, he was feeling sad that he wasn't in an intimate relationship and upset that he was down on people. He decided to sleep think the question, What's up with me and people? For some nights, he got nothing. Then he began to have quite lurid dreams that were a combination of science fiction and pornography. These dreams were fascinating and as good as any movies he'd ever seen, but when he tried to interpret them, he found that he couldn't penetrate their meaning, if indeed they had any.

These lively, arousing dreams continued and began to focus on an attractive coworker. But Mark had the sense that there was nothing to "interpret" here, that these were just sex fantasy dreams and didn't mean that he should ask his coworker out or even that he actually liked her. Happy enough with these dreams for their sexiness but unhappy that he wasn't getting closer to any self-knowledge, it occurred to him to change his sleep thinking question to Given that I don't like people that much, can I still have a decent life?

A few nights later a dream arrived that he knew was meaningful. It had to do with a young boy and an old man. The young boy, who had school books with him and appeared either to be on his way to school or maybe cutting school, was sitting on a high wall. An old man carrying an elaborately carved cane came down the road and passed below the boy, who called down to him in a friendly enough way—that was nevertheless a little sarcastic—"What's up, Grandfather?" The old man looked up at the boy and said, "You don't think I can read your tone of voice?" Something in the old man's direct look and rebuking words so affected the boy that he colored, got dizzy, and almost fell off the wall.

Mark knew that this was a meaningful dream. But he didn't know what it meant. It needed interpretation. But he had the insight that he couldn't begin by asking himself, "What does the high wall mean?" or "What does the carved cane mean?" He knew that he wouldn't get anywhere by dissecting the dream, by analyzing its symbols (if they were symbols), or by doing anything mechanical or formulaic. What he somehow needed to do was to hold the dream in its entirety and understand it in a holistic way. But what did *that* mean and how was he to accomplish it?

Mark sat at his desk, thinking. It occurred to him to ask himself the question, What arena does this dream feel like it's in? In the back of his mind, he had the idea that he could use this question to further sleep think the issue and suggest to his brain that it clarify the dream or offer the dream's message more directly. As he sat there, mulling this over, a thought came to him. He wondered whether anyone had ever mentored him. He wasn't sure whether he was on the right track with this thought, but he had the feeling that he might be. Finally, after sitting at his desk for more than hour, he got ready to go to work. While the dream remained uninterpreted, he had the sense that he was about to learn something or maybe that he had learned something already.

The next night, at about three in the morning, Mark was awakened by the following message: "You think no one has anything to teach you." He sat up and came fully awake. This message needed no interpreting. He knew exactly what it meant and exactly what it implied. He wrote down the following on his bedside pad: *Maybe not everyone is as stupid as you think. Maybe some people have things to offer you. That doesn't necessarily make them good or trustworthy. But it may make them your teachers. Maybe you need teachers of all sorts.*

Mark went back to bed. In the morning, the same ideas were still present. If anything, they were even clearer. He could sense that his first dreams were some mishmash of sexual desires and images from the high tech world in which he worked and not worth analyzing or even considering. But the "boy on the wall" dream was different, and while he couldn't make it reveal its secret, all he had to do was open to his own thoughts and feelings for its meaning to come to him. He understood that he had to think about people differently, that he had to moderate his feelings of superiority and take a genuine interest in people, as much for his sake as for theirs.

Within days, he began conversing with a woman at work who wasn't the youngest or the most beautiful but who, Mark recognized, seemed to have something important to teach him. Within a week, they had their first date planned.

Q. *I'm having real trouble interpreting the information I receive. I don't know what my dreams mean and I don't believe there's any mechanical way for me to know, for example, by using a dream analysis book or taking a class. I also can't tell what my sleep thoughts are worth. Even when a thought wakes me up and I write it down and then try to think about it the next morning, I usually can't tell what I'm supposed to do with the information or even what the information exactly is. It's really hard to know what I've got! What helps?*

Relaxing can help. Your questions reflect a worried state of mind and are like the questions I often get from creative clients who come in and say things such as "How can I know if the novel I'm writing is heading in the right direction?" or "How can I tell if my new film idea is a good one?" First, you have to relax and trust that you know what you need to know and that you have adequate evaluative capabilities built right into you. That isn't to say that you won't make mistakes; you will, and plenty of them. But still you need self-trust, a positive attitude, and a self-accepting way of being.

Second, you need to hone your evaluation skills. A practiced filmmaker can judge whether the music he's put on top of a scene is adding something to the scene or detracting from it. One filmmaker who specialized in horror films and always loaded on music, because the music made the scary scenes feel scarier, found that adding lots of music to scenes in his first "serious" movie made them feel overly sentimental. This is the kind of understanding that comes with practice, experience, conscious attention, and a desire to get things right. Stick with the process. You'll get progressively better at understanding what you're trying to tell yourself.

Jackie had a different sleep thinking experience from Mark. In her late 30s, employed as a paralegal, Jackie had done a lot of dream work in her life and regularly used the Tarot, the *I Ching*, psychics, astrological charts, and similar means to fathom her present and her future. She was used to interpreting signs, going with her intuitions, and finding meaning in a wrist ache, the look of the sky, or a chance remark.

At the moment, she was having problems with her 16-year-old daughter, Ashley. A single mom, Jackie worked late, came home tired, and didn't feel able to monitor her daughter as closely as she would have liked. In the past year, Ashley had come home drunk a few times—at least Jackie was pretty sure she'd been drunk—and her way of being—the clothes she wore, the look in her eyes, the look of her friends, her rebellious attitude—made Jackie suspect that Ashley was doing drugs. She alluded to the problem a few times and even confronted her directly once or twice, but Ashley just shrugged off her mom.

Jackie became more worried. Ashley was a high school sophomore, and her sophomore grades were going to count for college in a way that her first-year grades hadn't. The first semester of her sophomore year Ashley had done fairly well, but her interim spring report card grades had plummeted.

And she didn't seem to care. Jackie couldn't stand the idea of her daughter doing poorly and not even having a chance at a good college. She also felt strongly that this I-don't-give-a-damn attitude wasn't that of her real daughter but that of the school's antisocial, drug-using crowd.

The question most on her mind was whether or not she should search Ashley's room for drugs or evidence of drugs. She didn't like the idea of invading Ashley's privacy in that way, but she was beside herself with worry. She took the question to sleep think that very night: Should I search my daughter's room? During the night, she dreamt that she had searched Ashley's room and found a whole array of bizarre and dangerous things: a chain saw, a Bowie knife, hypodermic needles, and horrible-looking things that she couldn't identify. She awoke feeling that she had no choice but to search Ashley's room.

But she stopped herself. She realized that this was the answer she wanted in order to justify her actions, so she felt uncomfortable with the process. She had the distinct feeling that her brain had provided her with the very answer she demanded that it provide. She had the suspicion that she hadn't really been sleep thinking at all, that she had merely given herself justification for a search. She didn't feel good about acting on her "interpretation" of this dream; instead, she changed her sleep thinking question and took it to bed with her the next night.

Her new sleep thinking question was, What's the loving thing to do? That night nothing came to her, and she grew impatient and more worried, fearing that waiting was the worst answer. But she stuck with the process. The next night, again nothing came. She sat at her desk in the morning, hard pressed not to just stew about her daughter, and tried to use her writing prompts to bring forth something from the night.

But instead she wrote odd things that she supposed had nothing to do with Ashley, things about Ashley's dad and about her own childhood.

The third night she got a clear message, although it was only a single word: *arboretum*. She understood the reference; it was to the arboretum in the park where she'd taken Ashley for walks throughout Ashley's childhood years. But for a few seconds, she didn't understand the message. Then it came to her: She should walk with Ashley through the arboretum, not to interrogate her and not even to have a chat, but just to be with her daughter. When she suggested to Ashley that they spend some time together at the arboretum the following Saturday, Ashley surprised her by agreeing.

During their walk, Ashley confessed. She had been drinking and using marijuana. She wasn't sure if she was scared or whether she felt just fine about it, but she did know that she didn't like sneaking around and hiding things from her mother. She didn't pledge to stop, but she didn't dig in her heels, either. Instead, she left the door to stopping slightly ajar. For her part, it scared Jackie that the truth of the matter was that her daughter was using drugs, but it pleased her that she hadn't resorted to searching her room, which didn't feel honorable and which, had her daughter learned about it, might have caused a serious rift between them. What she knew for certain was that her sleep thinking had guided her to this walk in the arboretum, which was a great thing for the both of them.

Arnold, a sales rep for an electronics firm, was worried that he too had manipulated the sleep thinking process. He firmly believed that his wife was having an affair, hoped and prayed that he was wrong, and decided to take the question to bed to sleep think. It was odd to sleep think about his wife's infidelity with her next to him in bed, but still he managed to pose himself the question, Is Meg having an affair? And he was able to receive dreams that apparently answered his question. In each of the dreams, Meg flirted, got herself in compromising situations, and in other ways seemed to prove that she was being unfaithful. But each dream ended with Meg stopping short of intercourse. The dreams seemed to exonerate her.

But Arnold didn't believe his own dreams. He had the sense that the body of each dream was true but the conclusion false. He was watching the body of the dream as an observer but wishing the ending as its author, in accordance with his hope that Meg was being faithful to him. Arnold decided to surrender to his true understanding of his dreams and, with anguish, confusion, and pain, chose to sleep think a new question: What should I do?

There was no way he could pose this question as a wonder. In fact, he felt terrible asking it because he had the hunch that the only answers were to confront Meg or leave Meg, both of which terrified him. Still, he found the courage to sleep think his new question. But all that arrived the next few nights were tormenting dreams that, although they indicted Meg, seemed not to add anything meaningful to his understanding of the situation. Then, on the fifth night, he had a different sort of dream. In it, Meg and he were sitting at a small kitchen table in a cabin in the woods, the sun streaming in, and the birds chirping outside; they were having morning coffee together. In the dream, he asked Meg calmly, "Are you having an affair?" Meg replied, "Yes, but I'd like to stop." Arnold continued, "Well, when you do, we could talk." And Meg nodded and replied, "Thank you."

This dream made Arnold cry, but he wasn't sure whether the tears were tears of pain or tears of joy. He understood that he had to speak to Meg and that he had to speak to her exactly the way he'd spoken to her in the dream—not angrily, not defensively, not meekly, and not exactly matter of factly, although that phrase came closest to capturing his tone in the dream. In fact, he knew that he had to adopt exactly his dream tone and persona if he was going to save his marriage—which was what he hoped to do. It was no longer a question of whether Meg was having an affair or whether he could survive that news but rather what he would do with that news to best ensure that they had a chance of staying together.

Arnold had started out using his sleep thinking as a way to exonerate his wife and avoid the painful truth that she was having an affair. But he was honest enough to catch himself at his game. This is the very hardest work of the sleep thinking program: that is, remaining in right relationship with yourself so that you can think honestly and clearly about the issues that matter to you.

These three sleep thinkers each understood the basic rule of sleep thought interpretation: When something feels true, incline toward believing it, even though you have other evidence that apparently contradicts it and even though you wish it weren't true. Conversely, when something doesn't feel true, incline toward not believing it, even though it has supporting evidence and even though you wish it were true. Arnold could conjure up evidence that his wife was faithful and wished that she were faithful, but he was too honest to accept the dreams he'd manufactured to exonerate her. He looked more deeply, even though he didn't want to, and got better information, even though he hated receiving it.

Interpreting Your Sleep Thoughts

There are no rules or formulae for interpreting sleep thoughts. Just relax. Your brain provided you with this information. No doubt further information will also be available to you, either as you sit and mull over what you've received or as you sleep think the matter again.

Elaborate on the information you received in a few simple sentences. If, for example, you have the sense that your dream is suggesting that your chronic fatigue would be helped by an alternative therapy, such as acupuncture, write down what you're thinking as clearly as you can: *In the dream, I saw myself moving incredibly slowly. Then this Chinese woman came up to me and said something I couldn't quite understand. But I read in her eyes that she had knowledge of a way of healing me. Since I've been wanting to try acupuncture for my chronic fatigue, I take this dream to mean that I am more convinced than ever that I should see an acupuncturist.* If what you got was a feeling, try to put that feeling into words: *I woke up this morning feeling that I've been approaching my career all wrong. I've always thought that management wasn't for me, but now I think it might be just the right challenge, just the thing I need to keep me interested in what I'm doing.* If what you got was a thought or a message, first make sure you transcribe it accurately, then elaborate on it by using the prompt, "I think this means . . ." *I heard myself say, "Get out more." I think this means that although I spend all day with people at the office, I'm not actually spending any time with people who share my interests. I think "get out more" actually means "find some like-minded people to associate with."*

Mull over your interpretation. You may be absolutely right, you may be partially right, or you may be off target. Carry a small notepad with you, continue thinking about your interpretation during the day, and refine it, change it, or even reject it if some new thoughts occur to you. Even when you "know for sure" that you have an answer, don't close the door on further refinements and on further understanding. Even a seemingly complete answer is only a step in the process, not the final destination.

Think about whether you wish the information were true or whether you believe the information is actually true. We often get what we wish for from our brain. We may want to adopt a child and therefore get adoption dreams, but our wish may not be the whole story. We may want to move from a bustling city to a quieter locale, but the bucolic dreams that arrive may just be the expression of our wish, not a true indicator of the best course of action. Ask yourself, Is this information the fulfillment of a wish or the truth?

Let me elaborate on this point, since it is most important. You need to discover whether you are providing yourself, through your night work, with justification for doing something you already want to do, whether or not that's the best thing to do, or whether your night work has succeeded in overriding your wish fulfillment drive and is providing you with the most meaningful information. There is no place you can check this out except in your own heart and mind.

Surrender to your own knowing. The goal of sleep thinking is not to have your brain provide you with rehashed information or wish fulfillment information. The goal is to provide you with the most useful, truthful information possible. Ask your brain to be truthful, and then surrender to the fact that the truth it provides may make work for you, contradict what you supposed was true, or open up a can of worms.

There are no secrets to interpreting. You just sit each morning at your desk and process the night, thinking, recording, wondering, questioning yourself, and so on. The more you practice this, the better you will get at knowing what your thoughts mean and distinguishing their differences. During this morning hour of processing you will learn to decode the night's information—not because you have a code book but because you have a real willingness to under-stand yourself.

I hope that you've identified a problem to sleep think, crafted a prompt question, posed that question to yourself at bedtime, and experienced your brain focusing on that question during the night. I hope you've also gotten into the habit of going to your desk first thing each morning, before your "real" day begins, to attend to your sleep thoughts, inviting them forward, recording them, and thinking about them.

If you've done all this, you probably have some good clues concerning what to do about the problem you posed yourself. What remains is to actually do what your sleep thinking has suggested. The next chapter will help you think about how to get that work accomplished.

If you haven't yet reached the goals mentioned above, you might want to make a renewed effort. You now have all the information you need to get the sleep thinking program started. ((·))

6

CHAPTER

Making Changes

In this chapter we'll examine the remaining seven steps of the sleep thinking program:

Step 12. Make use of the information you receive.

Step 13. Plan for any necessary work or change.

Step 14. Accomplish the work and make the changes.

Step 15. Keep track of your progress.

Step 16. Sleep think new issues and questions.

Step 17. Bring sleep thinking fundamentals to your daytime thinking.

Step 18. Live an examined life.

If you've been working the sleep thinking program, you now have a variety of experiences under your belt. You've begun to look at your life in a more focused way, you've thought about the issues that concern you, and you've taken one of those issues to bed with you in order to better understand it. Information has begun to arrive—in your dreams, as thoughts, as images, as phrases—and you've taken the time each morning to try to understand what the information means. The next step is to learn how to make use of this information.

Make Use of the Information You Receive

How do you actually make use of the information you receive from your sleep thinking efforts? Let's say that you posed yourself the question, Why am I so unhappy? For several weeks, you sleep think that question and get all sorts of results: dreams about childhood, anxiety dreams, fragments of ideas, hunches, and so on. Then one morning you wake up and hear yourself say: "I shouldn't have gone into teaching." You don't have to interpret this information; you know exactly what you mean. You've had this thought a thousand times before. You know that you went into teaching because you loved history, not because you loved teaching. And in fact, you have never found being in a classroom anything but difficult. Because you've been sleep thinking, this recurrent thought has now returned with new clarity and new energy. Still, what are you to do with this information?

There are at least four things you can do:

1. Take a new sleep thinking question to bed. In this case, your next sleep thinking question might be, I know that I shouldn't have gone into teaching. But what am I supposed to do about that now? One of the things you can do

with the sleep thinking information you receive is simply to continue the sleep thinking process until you know what action to take.

2. Just think. Take the opportunity during your morning hour of processing and throughout the rest of the day to continue thinking about what you've learned and about what you still need to know. Consciously ask yourself the question, What am I supposed to do next? You can try to brainstorm answers or use the technique of "thinking in 20s" that I introduce later in this chapter. Because sleep thinking puts answers to your questions right on the tip of your tongue, you will be much closer to knowing what to do than you realize. All you need to do is to continue paying attention.

3. Bring forward what you already know you should do. Often what we receive from sleep thinking is information that we've known for a long time. For example, not only do we know that we're unhappy in our marriage, we know that we should leave it. Not only do we know that we should do a little fiction writing, we know what novel we want to write. What you can do with the information you receive from sleep thinking is be open to your own already formed conclusions, bring them into the light of day, and see if they hold up to scrutiny.

4. Ask for advice. You may not be in the habit of asking anyone for advice, so in order to get advice, you may first have to break through a mental block about asking. But if you can do that, you may begin to find that other people have ideas that haven't occurred to you or information that you don't possess. In our history teacher's case, he might get useful advice from his sister, a fellow teacher,

the school counselor, a career counselor, or even from his nephew John, who is only 9. Many others may have something useful to say to us. The great benefit of asking for advice can be simply hearing our ideas out loud.

Of these four methods our history teacher—let's call him Bill—tries brainstorming. As has happened before, he feels pretty defeated before he starts, because part of him doesn't believe that he has any real options. Forty is not old but it is not an age where he can see learning new technologies and joining the information revolution, starting out in some company that has great retirement benefits but that demands sixty hours a week from him, or launching some home business which he might enjoy but which might never pay anything. In short, he has thought about this before and feels pretty gloomy before he starts. But still he wills himself to brainstorm.

Because he's gotten into the habit of sitting at his desk early each morning to process his thoughts, he finds it easier than usual to think about his problem, even though some gloominess is present. "All right," he says to himself, "I shouldn't have gone into teaching. Now what?" He opens himself up to possible answers and brainstorms the following list of possibilities:

-)) Become a stock day trader.
-)) Relax. Teaching isn't so bad.
-)) Try another school.
-)) Go into the fence building business.
-)) Become a lawyer.
-)) Write a book on the gypsies.
-)) Relax. Try to enjoy teaching.
-)) Retire early. Somehow.
-)) Go into administration.

)) Give up. Live on the street.

)) Retire early. Write.

)) Teach fewer classes. Somehow. Teach part-time.

)) Rob a cyber bank.

)) Spend 20 years with a corporation.

)) Learn a new skill fast. Become a . . . something.

)) Just teach. Make teaching more fun. Somehow.

)) Write . . . and teach. Really start a book.

)) Have breakfast.

Bill looks over his list. Suddenly he gets a picture of what he actually wants. He wants to retire early—at fifty-five—and write books. He even knows which books he wants to write. He has the ambition to write about the history of Central Europe from the point of view of the gypsies, a multivolume series that would start in antiquity and come up to the present. He's wanted to do this for years, but he's never come close to beginning. Suddenly, he has the sense that he might begin, that he might live his dream.

Getting information is a vital part of the process, but only part of the process. Even a clear message such as "I shouldn't have gone into teaching" isn't enough information, although it may be the truth and an important insight. You still have to figure out how to make use of the news. Bill always knew that he needed more from life than teaching. This information was known to him for 15 years. But until he tried sleep thinking, he didn't know what to do with this information. Now he did, at least in a starting way. Somehow he would retire early, and somehow he would become a nonfiction writer specializing in the gypsies of Europe.

Plan for Any Necessary Work or Change

Bill has reached a decision. He has decided that he is going to retire early and write history books, starting now and continuing after his retirement from teaching. But that is quite a mouthful! He has little savings, the tiniest pension plan at work, and slim prospects of retiring early. Nor has he ever written a book. These are such daunting difficulties that no one would be surprised if Bill shook his head and said to himself, "Nice dream. Back to my lesson planning."

The things we want to accomplish are often this large, scary, and daunting. It is easy to become frightened and stop thinking about them. Many messages go through our head, often right at the edge of conscious awareness so that they duck in and out of consciousness, messages such as "I can't make that happen" or "There's no chance." Because we're plagued by such messages, it's crucial that we formally plan for anything we want, making to-do lists, schedules, and mechanical things of that sort, and really identify what steps will be necessary in order for us to achieve our goals. Planning helps counteract our fear and our negativity.

Most people don't do enough planning. Not only don't they plan adequately for some of the more obvious long-term goals in their life, like saving for a house down payment, their children's education, or their own retirement, but they are even less in the habit of making plans for their short-term goals. They may say, "I'd like to write a book," but they don't sit down for a minute and make a plan of attack for getting that book written. Instead they say, "Maybe I'll get inspired one day and then I'll begin writing." Or they want to change an aspect of their personality; they may, for example, want to learn to trust themselves more or become more disciplined. But they don't sit down and create a plan for becoming more disciplined. Instead, they tell themselves that they aren't disciplined enough to plan.

Thinking in 20s

A great way to help construct a useful plan for any course of action is to "think in 20s." By this I mean that instead of saying to yourself, "What's the one thing I can do to quit smoking (or end this abusive relationship, improve my flute playing, become a more confident person, etc.)?" you say, "What are 20 things I might try?"

This is an extremely liberating exercise. Instead of worrying that you may not be able to come up with just the right thing, you relax and allow yourself to think of lots of potential actions. For instance, imagine that you want to stop smoking. Instead of stopping at your first thought, say, to try nicotine gum or maybe to give hypnosis a shot, you let yourself dream up 20 possibilities, without censoring yourself or worrying about whether you are being ridiculous. As a result, you have a much richer array of choices. Here's a sample list:

1. Keep count of every cigarette I smoke and smoke one fewer each day.

2. Tape pictures of my infant daughter to my cigarette case, to remind myself that I won't be there for her wedding.

3. Smoke only cigarettes that I can't easily find, like gold-banded Egyptians.

4. Put up pictures of dying smokers all over the house.

5. Try nicotine gum.

6. Join Smokers Anonymous.

7. Write a letter to my daughter, telling her why smoking was so important to me.

8. Stop worrying about weight gain—in fact, set out to gain 20 pounds.

9. Try sugarless gum.

10. Figure out for myself if anything can short-circuit a craving.

11. Think about whether I want to live.

12. Try hypnosis.

13. Only smoke when it rains (and move to the desert).

14. Learn to think "don't need it" whenever I think "cigarette."

15. Get angry at myself, really angry.

16. Tell my wife to start nagging me.

17. Change my mind about there being no life after cigarettes.

18. Try self-hypnosis.

19. Tell everybody, even perfect strangers, that only idiots smoke.

20. Just stop.

Not only do you end with more possibilities by creating a list of this sort, but the act of compiling it makes you aware in a deeper way of the obstacles confronting you and your reasons for charting a new course of action.

Planning is just an everyday way to organize tasks, keep track of your goals, get things done one step at a time, and know what you're doing next. The hardest part about it is the anxiety that wells up when you think about planning.

In Bill's case, it makes him terribly anxious to think about retirement, since he's sure there's no way he can retire early, and doubly anxious when he thinks about writing a book, an endeavor that feels far beyond his capabilities. But still, following the program, he sits down with two sheets of paper and titles one "early retirement" and the other "book on gypsies." Just sitting there with these two sheets makes him so anxious that he has to make himself another cup of coffee. But when his coffee is ready, he returns to the blank sheets of paper and begins.

On the first sheet he writes:

How much will I need? (Oh God, I don't want to know. What about inflation? Maybe I'll need a million dollars a year to live in a hovel.)

What will my tiny school annuity amount to? (I think if I tell them a projected amount, they will tell me what I would get monthly. So I'll have to project what I could put away over the next 15 years and how much that would earn.)

Where will I live? (I can't live here. It's too expensive. I should start thinking about where I might live. . . someplace that's cheap. . . and sunny. . . and interesting.)

This isn't a plan yet, but it's approaching one. You can see how a plan might emerge quickly. Bill might begin by figuring out where he'll retire to, which is a complicated decision in its own right, but until he knows that, he may not be able to gauge how much money he'll need to live on. So the first part of his plan might be making a list of criteria for his retirement locale, thinking about that list, researching some retirement possibilities in books or on the Internet, and sleep thinking the question, Where do I want to retire? Maybe he'll discover that he is well suited to retiring in Italy, or Costa Rica, or North Dakota. If something clicks, Bill will have made significant progress. If nothing clicks, he can continue to devote some time each week to thinking about retirement locales and researching possibilities.

On the second sheet of paper, the one for his book on gypsies, he writes:

How do you write a book? (Oh God. Do I have to take some stupid workshops? Or buy books on writing books? Or take a class? Or join a writing group?)

Maybe everything's been done. I should look on Amazon and see what there is.

What would my book—or books—be about? I know a lot about gypsy life, but what do I want to say? Do I have anything to say? Wait, that's getting negative. Let me stay positive. I need to discover what I want to say about gypsy life. Maybe I'll only know that once

I begin writing, or maybe I can figure it out beforehand. Beforehand would be nice!

This, too, isn't a plan yet, but it has the makings of a plan. The logical first step is to see what's been written about gypsies. When Bill logs onto Amazon and plugs in the subject word *gypsy*, scores of titles appear. But as he glances over the titles, he finds that the list isn't daunting. Most of the books are out of print or hard to find. Some sound very academic and deadly dull. Some sound interesting but are narrowly focused, on the gypsies of Russia, the fate of gypsies during the Holocaust, one gypsy's personal adventure, and so on. Bill grows excited. He begins to see how his book, about which he knows nothing yet, might meet an actual need, one not met by the books his search has unearthed.

Accomplish the Work and Make the Changes

There is good news and bad news about change. The bad news is that change can be extremely difficult. The good news is that even though it can be difficult, it is still possible if you truly want it, it is a human-sized change, and you prepare yourself for growth.

We may desire a thing but also desire its opposite. For example, we may want to stop smoking but also want the benefits of smoking; we may want to write a romance but also want to avoid the pain of writing a bad romance; or we may want to start a risky home business but also want to retain the security of our paycheck. This is how it is with so many things we want; we want it and its opposite. This dilemma is known as conflictual desire. It is very hard to change until the conflict is resolved. A person needs to be able to say, "I want to stop smoking, *and* I no longer need the benefits of smoking." "I want to write a romance, *and* I do not fear writing a bad romance." "I want to start a home business, *and* I do not care about a regular paycheck." When we no longer desire those things that contradict and inhibit our stated desire, then we *really* desire it and can finally have it.

Such readiness almost always precedes change. Somewhere just out of conscious awareness we ready ourselves to, say, leave our lover, quit drinking, start writing our novel, change careers, or go back to school. Sleep thinking helps you accomplish this preparatory work. It increases your readiness by helping you think, both during the night and during your morning processing, about what you really want to accomplish. Sleep thinking helps you to keep your eye on the ball.

Therefore, the further good news about change is that it is not always difficult. Since you may be ready, the change may come effortlessly. Something that on Monday you did not think you could possibly do, such as sign up for a digital photography class, on Friday you find perfectly easy and natural to do. There's no exact accounting for this sudden ease, and readiness may only be a partial answer. But the inner experience is like a switch being thrown. One minute the switch is locked in the down position and change feels impossible. The next minute some inexplicable shift occurs, and we feel less afraid; the locking mechanism releases, and the switch throws itself. And suddenly, we manage to accomplish a hitherto impossible change effortlessly.

Keep Track of Your Progress

There is something very satisfying about keeping track of our progress in life. While it is beyond our abilities to keep track of everything we think, feel, and do, it's altogether possible to keep track of individual threads of our life fabric. This is what a scientist does as she keeps track of a central idea from experiment to experiment and what a novelist does with each of his novels. But few people keep track of personal issues in such a consistent, diligent way.

If you regularly keep a journal or a diary, you may be used to doing this sort of tracking. But most journal writing is of the free association sort, with each day bringing a new focus and a new emphasis. It's rare for even a practiced diarist to start out each day articulating her progress on a single issue. But this is important work to do, because the act of tracking your progress helps you maintain the intention to change in the face of the new obstacles, lingering doubts, failures of will, and other challenges that inevitably arise when we try to make important changes in our life.

You may want to keep individual notebooks for each sleep thinking issue you tackle. In your individual notebook, you might summarize your progress every few days, writing as little as a few sentences or as much as whole pages. This summarizing is different work from your morning hour of processing. That morning hour is when you receive thoughts that were produced during the night, make new connections, solve and resolve issues, and create. It is when you have realizations, revelations, and epiphanies. Your summarizing work, on the other hand, is a time of cool reflection. You consider how well or poorly you've been doing, whether you've been able to make the changes you outlined for yourself, and so on. Out of this summary work come new sleep thinking questions and new ideas for tactics and strategies to help you stay on track. The primary goal of summarizing is to record as honestly as you can what's transpired with respect to a particular issue since you last summarized your progress.

Because processing and summarizing are different tasks and serve different purposes, you may want to process in the morning but keep track in the evening. While your goal is to process every day, weekends included, you can keep track of your progress more irregularly, say every several days. You want latitude in this regard because nothing much may happen for a couple of days. You may have no particular progress to note. If you think you have to record your progress every day but don't have much to say, you'll begin to feel like you're failing. So it makes sense to process regularly but to summarize only when necessary. But you shouldn't let too many days go by. You shouldn't begin to say to yourself, "As soon as I have something important to put down, I'll get my summary notebook out." Consider four days about as long as you'll want to go without summarizing.

Q. *Is it possible to get the wrong answers from sleep thinking? Could I be led astray?*

Of course. Unfortunately, your brain doesn't come with a money-back guarantee. It is a grand but not perfect organ, and it is guided not just by biology but also by psychology. You may have reasons for giving yourself the wrong answer. You may have reasons for avoiding the right answer. You may have conflicting internal agendas. In fact, you can be certain that you do. Everyone does. As stated earlier, someone may want to stop smoking yet not want to give up the benefits of smoking. When you try to sleep think a plan to stop smoking, which part of you will do the sleep thinking? Will it be the part that needs the nicotine and gets comfort from smoking or the part that wants to be healthy and not get lung cancer? Someone in an abusive relationship who is also dependent on her spouse for money both wants to leave but also has powerful motivation to stay put. Which part of her will end up sleep thinking the question, Should I leave my husband?

But if you follow the steps of the program, process your thoughts every morning, and enter into a relationship with yourself that is open, truthful, and genuine, you have a good chance of avoiding missteps and providing yourself with answers that are in your best interest.

Sleep Think New Issues and Questions

Mark, a painter in his mid-30s, had been sleep thinking creative projects for years. He virtually always went to bed with his current painting on his mind, and because he used sleep thinking so effectively, he'd become a very productive artist. He also took problems to bed to sleep think, and from this work, he'd changed himself from a reluctant marketer of his work to a person comfortable with the demands of the marketplace. Through sleep thinking, he'd even found a way to make peace with his father, who'd never really forgiven him for choosing painting over the family business.

For a time, nothing pressing was on Mark's mind. Yet beneath the surface was a pressing issue that never went away as a concern. That issue was his sexual orientation. He dated women, but he felt attracted to men, and just recently, he'd felt himself attracted to a man in so powerful a way that the issue was moving right into the forefront of his consciousness. He knew that he had to tackle it; his whole body was demanding that he make up his mind about who he was and what he intended to do.

It seemed to him preposterous that he could be in his mid-30s and not know who he was. Yet that was the truth. It was also the truth that he felt so many internal and external pressures that it was very hard to know anything about his sexual makeup with clarity. He dated women and slept with them, but he wasn't convinced that that was who he was. He felt attracted to men, but only occasionally, so that wasn't clear either. When he thought of himself as gay, he balked, and when he thought of himself as straight, he didn't really believe it. He supposed that made him bisexual, but that label didn't clear up his confusion or feel any more satisfactory than the labels "gay" or "straight."

He took the matter to bed. The question he posed himself was, Who am I? Just as he expected he would, he experienced night after night of turbulent, nightmarish dreams. None of the dreams felt as if they clarified matters. They seemed to repeat what he already knew: that he could sleep with women, but that men really attracted him, though in a dangerous way. He knew that he could interpret his dreams as meaning that he was afraid to give himself over to homosexuality, but to interpret them that way seemed to add nothing to what he already knew.

Then he tried a new question: What's in the way? His dreams changed. Suddenly they were about his mother and father. There were strange dreams of family parties unlike any that had actually occurred, parties at which the guests would talk about gays in every way imaginable, from the most accepting and flattering to the most rejecting and cruel. His mother seemed not to want to hear what was being said and wandered around offering tidbits and drinks and smiling a hostess smile. His father took every opportunity to lambaste gays. He recognized this cruel streak in his father and he knew that his father was homophobic, but he had never seen it played out this way, so completely.

Mark realized that his father's homophobia and his mother's potential disappointment were such powerful obstacles to thinking of himself as gay that he couldn't really get past them. It struck him that he had to address his concerns about his parents before he could learn anything more about himself. So he chose a new sleep thinking question: What about my parents?

It took about a month, but one night he had an important dream. In it, he saw himself in the house in which he grew up, in his own room, listening to his parents fight. They were fighting about something that didn't concern him at all, but the barely repressed violence between them affected him deeply. He'd had no conscious idea that all that violence was lurking just beneath the surface, and suddenly he understood that he feared his parents at a visceral level. He was simply afraid of them, and that was why he couldn't tell them things they didn't like hearing.

Right on the heels of this insight came the clear understanding that he was gay, a truth he'd been scared to acknowledge. He didn't know how—or whether—he'd tell his parents, but he did know that he could now begin to live his life.

Bring Sleep Thinking Fundamentals to Your Daytime Thinking

You can train yourself to accomplish the equivalent of sleep thinking while you're awake. But you must master these few crucial steps for this to happen:

» Quiet your mind.
» Manage your anxiety.
» Maintain a here-and-now orientation.
» Have a prompt and a direction.
» Surrender to thought.

These aren't sequential steps but rather a complete mind-set that kicks in whenever you want to think about something or whenever you want to create. Let's imagine that our history teacher, Bill, has begun his book on gypsies and has some idea of what it's about. At first he only works on it evenings. But then, as the book becomes more interesting to him, he finds that he is compelled to work on it at school, too, during his breaks. But for several weeks, he finds that he can't do it. When his breaks come, he continues grading papers, maybe reads a magazine, or just shuts his eyes.

Then one day he devises a small personal mantra: "My gypsy book. My gypsy book." The meaning of his mantra is this: "My gypsy book has become very important to me, and I want to be thinking about it all the time, whenever I'm not obligated to think about other things." He tries this mantra out during his morning break at school and finds himself drifting away from his school mind and entering an open space that begins to fill with thoughts about his book. He writes for a bit, and when he looks up, 20 minutes have passed and his break is over. Two pages of his book are done.

During his break, Bill went deep into a place that is very like NREM sleep, a place characterized by its silence and separation from the everyday world. Privacy is not necessary to reach this place. Only social anxiety prevents us from engaging in daytime sleep thinking. Usually, we are too concerned about how we look to think in public. But once Bill got used to thinking about his book at school, it wasn't much of a leap to begin thinking about it in the teachers' lounge as well as in his own office.

He soon discovered that teachers coming and going and even the occasional question directed his way didn't distract him very much. He would nod, smile, and go right back to his thoughts. He imagined that he was beginning to resemble an absent-minded physicist who never stopped working on some problem, a painter who could set up an easel in a crowd and paint unselfconsciously, or a writer who could sit at a coffee house table and write all day long, not caring that his one cup of coffee was all the rent he was paying. Bill realized that he was becoming creative.

Live an Examined Life

Plato quotes his teacher Socrates as arguing that an unexamined life is not worth living. But that is extremely hard to actually do! In fact, some scholars believe that Socrates himself failed to understand how to save himself when he was arrested for blasphemy and forced to commit suicide.

The people of his time revered free speech, at least in principle. Yet Socrates never once argued in his defense that his accusers were depriving him of this principle of liberty. Of course, he may have thought that such an argument would fall on deaf ears and that his accusers' minds were made up. But what if Socrates was simply too proud to condescend to argue on his own behalf? What if Socrates himself couldn't adequately see into his own nature at such a critical moment in his life?

Living an examined life is hard for everyone, maybe Socrates included. But the sleep thinking program can help you live your life more consciously. The skills you're learning—how to manage anxiety so that you can think more clearly, how to prompt yourself down a line of thought by asking relevant questions, how to analyze your own thoughts so as to determine what you want to do next—are the skills of the self-aware person. Just as love is an idle word if one doesn't engage in loving actions, so self-awareness is an idle idea unless one actually practices it, taking time and making the effort to look in the mirror. The sleep thinking program is a way to take that time and make that effort.

Not much in our daily life supports the goal of examining our motives and actions. At work, we have an endless stream of tasks to accomplish. Very much the same is true at home. Even our spiritual traditions provide us more with rules and rituals than with a demand that we think for ourselves. Sleep thinking is a way to realize your intention of living an examined life.

Q. *Do I have to follow the steps of the sleep thinking program in order to get results?*

There are no rules or "shoulds" connected to sleep thinking. I'm advising you to do certain things, such as prepare an initial list of sleep thinking questions and go to bed with a particular question in mind, but you can sleep think without posing yourself any questions and without doing any "work" at all. All you need to do is believe that your thoughts are important and that you want your projects to succeed and your problems to be resolved. In short, you only need to do one thing: Maintain the right attitude. If you take yourself seriously and plan to use your brain while you sleep, it will do just that.

Although there are no rules or "shoulds," I do believe that it helps to approach sleep thinking in an organized way. It is hard to write a book if you don't work on it each day. It is hard to sell your business ideas to investors without a business plan. It is hard to accomplish anything if you don't do it regularly and in an organized fashion. You can certainly create your own version of the sleep thinking program and proceed in your own way, and you can certainly benefit from sleep thinking without working any sort of program. But you will probably only get the results you want if you work toward them with some regularity and organization.

You now have a sense of what sleep thinkers do. They learn from themselves, reflect on what they've learned, and decide what specific actions to take. They pencil these actions into their day—a conversation with their son right after work, an hour at the library in the evening to research a new career—and make accomplishing those actions a top priority. By spending an hour first thing every morning reaping the fruits of their sleep thinking and by transforming what they've learned into action, they become more decisive, masterful, and empowered.

Now that you've read through the 18 steps, think about whether you want to circle back and start your own sleep thinking adventures. If you're already working the program, congratulations! Let's continue then. ((·))

Solving Your Problems

Let's begin our investigation of how to solve your problems while you sleep with five stories from individuals who weren't working the sleep thinking program, but who, like each of us, had the experience of using their brain at night in their own behalf.

Jennifer's Story

When I was 15 years old, my Aunt Betty died of breast cancer. She was 33. From the time I was a baby, my aunt spent a lot of time with me. She took me to the park, to movies, to bookstores, and for long walks. I grew up talking with her and confiding in her and asking her for advice when I had problems.

Betty was diagnosed with cancer when she was 28 and was told that she only had 6 months to live. She kept a positive attitude, and when she talked with me, she spoke as if she would be with me forever. I was afraid of losing her and afraid that I would be unable to solve my problems without her.

Betty fought the disease for five years but finally lost the battle. I was devastated and felt all alone. I just knew that no one could understand me and, therefore, that no one could help me. I was 15 years old and about to encounter the toughest years of my young life.

A few months after Betty died, I began to experience social problems at school. I spent time with the popular crowd and was beginning to experience peer pressure. I was afraid to tell my parents, and I didn't know if I should stand up to my friends. My emotions were out of control, and I couldn't think clearly. I didn't know what to do, but I felt as though I were running out of time.

One night, in the midst of my turmoil, I had a dream. I was standing in a house that was of gold-colored clay. There were windows with no glass and a doorway with no door. The house consisted of one big room and felt very open and airy. The sky outside was blue, with a few billowy white clouds, and I could feel a light breeze around me.

The room was very sparsely furnished, with only a bed, a small table, and two or three small pictures. The bed-spread was white, and the floor was the same gold-colored clay as the walls.

Suddenly, I was sitting on the side of the bed, and Betty was facing me. It did not startle me at all. We were just there, as if we'd magically appeared. I felt very peaceful. Betty began to talk to me, and she explained why the kids at school were pressuring me to do things I knew were wrong. She told me what a strong, smart and admirable person I was, and I could almost feel how much she meant what she was saying. She told me exactly what to say to the kids who were pushing me and described the ways each one might react.

As suddenly as Betty appeared in my dream, she was gone. I felt calm, secure, strong, and at peace. I sat for a while, and then the dream ended. I had the most amazing feeling when I awoke. At that time, I believed that Betty actually visited me in my dream.

As I got older, I thought those words of wisdom were actually my own conscience telling me the right thing to do. Somewhere in the back of my mind, I knew that the side of me that attended school every day did not trust my own instincts and that I would believe the words if they came from Betty, my longtime companion, trusted confidant, and loved one.

Whatever the source, my dream helped me to solve a problem that could have become very serious. The consequences of my actions, had I not listened to my dream, would have resulted in serious repercussions.

This is one way that sleep thinking works. Your own brain figures out how to send you a message *that you will hear*, since it cannot seem to get through to you during the day. What this means, of course, is that in a corner of conscious awareness, you know that you have an answer to your own problem, but you can't seem to make yourself listen to your own answer while you're awake. So, under the cover of darkness, you create a scenario that will convince you, say, by having your answer provided by a trusted loved one who is no longer living.

Is there someone, living or dead, who could help you solve your current problem, someone whom you'd like to get advice from or discuss things with? Invite that person to visit you while you sleep. Try it out this very night, using as your sleep thinking

> prompt an invitation such as "I'd love to visit with
> you, Jim" or "Can you help me out, Mom?"

Another feature of sleep thinking is that it allows you to
predict. In this case, Jennifer "was told" how each of her
friends would react when she informed them that she wasn't
interested in their out-of-bounds activities. These predictions
are not premonitions or psychic experiences of any sort. It is
simply that your brain has the ability to analyze past experiences and surmise that, for example, if you tell Mary something she doesn't want to hear, she will probably insult you
and try to make your life miserable; if you tell Lillian something she doesn't want to hear, she'll act like she's deaf and
shun you.

That it wasn't really Betty speaking and that Jennifer
didn't receive the information in any psychic way in no way
lessened its value, for it was surely Jennifer's best available
information of the moment. It was simply presented to her in
a fashion that her brain—that is, that she herself—thought
would be most compelling.

> Is there something you need to predict, for example,
> how someone will react or what will happen when
> you try out a new thing? Use as your sleep thinking
> prompt, I wonder what will happen when _____

Trish's Story

This whole year has been a time of financial turmoil. But
things suddenly got worse. It sounds so silly, but it began
like this. I had no stamps and my bills were already delin-
quent. In addition, I had lost my on-line banking code. For

days, I vowed to call, after my search for the missing banking code had proved fruitless. But by the time I remembered to call each day, it was always after banking hours. I told myself that the bank was closed—even though no doubt there was an 800 number—and that I would have to wait until the next day, during normal business hours.

Day after day went by and I could not—or would not—contact my bank. My work was stressful, and I had to work long hours. Every day at 5 P.M., I told myself, "It's too late to call." Every night I tossed and turned, worrying about paying my bills. Then, one afternoon, I was informed at work that I would be laid off. I felt immediately depressed and went into denial about my future. That night, I couldn't get to sleep until the wee hours of the morning. But then I had a dream that saved me.

My recollection is a bit foggy now, but I'll try to explain. In my dream, I warned myself of the consequences of not paying my bills and I told myself to act responsibly. It felt as though I were speaking to just a shell of myself; it was as if my body were broken. I woke right up. It was about 5:30 in the morning. I went straight to the computer, logged on-line, found the number, and called. To my amazement somebody answered. He helped me establish a new password. By doing that I was able to log on to the computer and set up the payments for my bills. Everything ended up okay. I got my bills paid, and I even got a new job very quickly.

That dream was basically a wake-up call for me. I had to take care of my responsibilities because they wouldn't just go away. I got myself out of depression and am standing firmly on both feet now. I have learned that it is best to tackle a situation head-on as soon as it arises, rather than let it fester and take control of me.

It wouldn't have been surprising if Trish had remembered where her account number was hidden or even if she remembered the number itself, because when you sleep think, you often retrieve lost information. You can retrieve lost information of an ordinary sort—where your car keys are, where that missing bill is that you can't seem to find—but you can also retrieve much more vital information. You can remember the melody that vanished that you need for the song you're writing. You can remember the conversation with your stepfather that helps you understand why you had that falling out so long ago and why you had to leave home. It's impossible to know if every piece of "lost" information has been saved somewhere in memory, but information returns so regularly to the practiced sleep thinker that it's safe to assume that very little that we experience is ever completely lost.

> Is there something you've been wanting to recall? In bed tonight, make a point of asking yourself directly, What really happened the night Mark came home drunk? or What was that great idea I had for a short story?

Trish's story, like Jennifer's, also shows how sleep thinking works. Sometimes a problem results because of the pressures we're facing. We aren't happy with the path we're taking, and we manage to "slip" under the pressures, until sleep thinking works to give us a warning.

> Is there something about your own behavior that's bothering you, something you know you shouldn't have done or should stop doing? See if you can bring the matter up tonight.

Yolanda's Story

My problem started in August of this year. I had just come back from visiting the West Indies. I had done an exhaustive search on my father's parents and grandparents' roots and had found some of the data that I was looking for. While I was still in the West Indies, I broke down and cried from joy. I was happy to be there, and I was also happy to discover my roots. But there were other things going on, too. I have never truly gotten over the death of Marvin, my cousin. Going back to the West Indies reawakened my thoughts about all the hurt and rejection that he must have suffered, for being gay and having AIDS, when we were there together years before.

Then, during the months of September and October, more devastating things happened. My friend Wanda died. Then my car broke down. I had wanted to go back to college, but I couldn't get there without transportation. I live only eight blocks from work, so I could always walk to the office, but my dream of going to college seemed ruined. I signed up for school anyway, but then I was rejected for my lack of writing skills (I've been accepted since). Too much was happening!

Then, just a few days ago, my daughter came to my home to visit. She commented on how cold it was, how dark it was, and the fruit flies in the kitchen. I felt that she was overreacting by leaving after just two minutes. But it must have made an impression on me. When I went to sleep, I felt so tired. But I woke up feeling much better. I knew that I must have worked something out during the night because things just came clear to me. I didn't recall any dreams or anything of that sort, but surely something had happened.

As I thought about my experiences of the previous four months, I realized that I had been in a state of depression—and now I was going to come out of it. I realized that my apartment was dark; 18 light bulbs had burned out, and I'd been in no rush to replace them. The fruit flies were from dishes that had gone unwashed for a long time. I believe that I had just stopped caring. My home lacked the love and attention that I had previously lavished on it. I realized that I had intentionally closed myself off from visitors. I realized that I was still functioning, but no more than that.

I've learned from this to spot the signs of depression. I will open up my heart and learn to love and care again. I will grieve, I will laugh, I will express joy, I will fight my depression and move forward, and I will replace those 18 light bulbs!

Very often we don't recognize what mood we're in, even if our mood is with us around the clock and is coloring everything that we do. It's possible to be depressed for months and even years and not know it. After, for example, a divorce, a death, or our last child leaving for college, we may experience a low-grade depression that never lets up. But because it doesn't incapacitate us, it never shows its face clearly.

We keep living right through the depression, busying ourselves, cooking, watching television, and all the rest, not noticing that we never smile, that nothing is pleasurable, and that everything about life feels arduous and has a gray tone to it. But hints about our mood and even direct announcements that we're depressed (or furious, upset, anxious, and so on) can and do come to us when we sleep. During the night, we can "work out" what's bothering us and wake up feeling much better.

Use sleep thinking to check in on your moods and to improve them. Whenever you feel a little depressed or blue, try sleep thinking on the question, What would make me feel better? or What would help change my mood?

Suzanne's Story

I solved a personal problem last Christmas that I have been agonizing over every Christmas and Mother's Day for the past three years. My problem was whether or not to continue sending obligatory Christmas and Mother's Day cards to my birth mother, Sarah Jane. We stopped speaking and corresponding in 1995 after we had our first ever-real fight.

She had to come to California for a visit and stayed with me, as she had in previous years. For some reason, this trip was filled with tension and unspoken feelings. She exploded at me in the middle of the very busy lobby of the Kabuki Theater in San Francisco, after we had seen a movie together. She very loudly declared me the most selfish person she knew. The car ride back to my apartment was silent. I dropped her off and called a friend to cool off. Sarah Jane packed her things and stayed at an old friend's house for the duration of the visit.

I knew that we had issues to deal with, but I wasn't prepared to deal with them at the theater. We had a long cooling off period after that and then the holidays came. I am the type of person who loves to buy the perfect box of Christmas cards and write special notes to my friends and distant family. I look forward to it every year.

I put on some warm flannel pajamas, make some hot tea, grab my new box of cards and the Rolodex, jump into bed, and then spread out the cards in front of me. But every year since my fight with Sarah Jane, I struggle when I get to her card. I signed my name and my son Alec's name on the card the first year after our fight, but only Alec's name has appeared on the cards since then.

Last year was especially hard because I didn't understand what the silence from her end meant. She had stopped sending me birthday and Christmas cards, and I was feeling resentful that I had tried to keep up the connection and she hadn't. I stopped when I came to Sarah Jane's name. I decided I would not send her one. Then I fell asleep.

In my sleep, I heard a voice. It wasn't a dream; it was just someone speaking. I don't know whose voice it was, but it wasn't mine, and it wasn't Sarah Jane's. The voice said, "Send her the card. One day it'll help when you tell Alec everything." I think I heard the same message several times during the night. I could tell, even in my sleep, that I was resistant to the message, because I was really angry with Sarah Jane. But when I awoke I said to myself, "I can be bigger and better than she is. I'm going to send her a card—and a really nice message." And I did just that. I don't know what it will mean, if anything, but I felt right doing it. I don't think it would have felt good acting as petty as Sarah Jane was acting.

Suzanne knew that she wanted nothing more to do with her mother, but she discovered through sleep thinking that she shouldn't let her anger and resentments stop her from doing what was best. She learned that it might be wise to maintain some sort of contact, for the sake of Alec and maybe for her own sake as well. She couldn't resolve this conflict during her waking hours; she couldn't even articulate it. So she did some sleep thinking on it and came up with the solution that best served her.

> Very often the problems we have result from a con-
> flict between two true things, for example, that we
> want our mother to visit but that we also need some
> time to ourselves, that we want to perform but that
> we're also made anxious by performing, or that we
> don't want to put too much pressure on our child but
> that we want her to be very successful. Such a con-
> flict may be simmering in you right now. To find out,
> try one of these sleep thinking prompts: Am I caught
> on the horns of some dilemma? or Is there some con-
> flict raging in me that I'm not even aware of?

Wendy's Story

When I first met my husband, Walter, I was going through an extremely hard time in my life. My sister had died earlier in the year, and a close friend was gravely ill. I'd also broken off a relationship with a fellow after dating him for three years. I needed a mental health break and was not really ready to make a commitment to a new person.

Walter must have realized this because he didn't push our relationship. He took me to the hospital every day to see my friend Rachel, who was dying, and he was there for me after she passed away. A few months later, after we had met for our Wednesday night pizza together, he asked me if I could see a future for the two of us. I dodged his question and forgot about it for a while.

One night, while sleeping, the whole scenario of a relationship with Walter played itself out in my mind. It wasn't like dreaming, exactly, it was much more like visualizing something or watching two people on a stage doing improv. I could tell that I was really trying to bring up things and get them answered. I'd tell Walter about a problem with my parents, who are old and in another state, and he'd answer me. It went on like that. It was like an interview or a test. And Walter passed! He passed with flying colors. So I felt good about telling him that, yes, we should get married.

This is a terrific example of sleep thinking. It shows very clearly how active, forward-looking, and smart our brain can be when it is free to think. Faster than any computer, it can imagine situations and judge from the information it has how people will react in those situations. It can test hypotheses and measure people. It can play out all the twists and turns in a relationship. It can imagine what two people will do in brand-new situations, given their personalities. It can tell you how each person in your family will react at Thanksgiving to the secret you're thinking of revealing.

If your brain could not solve problems of this sort, creativity would be impossible. Every novelist would find himself stuck putting his characters in a situation and then not knowing how to proceed, except by hiring live people who resemble his characters and having them play out the situation. But novelists don't have to do that and neither do you. Our brain is terrific at just that sort of thinking, and it does its best work when the lights are out and quiet descends on the household.

Solving Problems Just by Thinking

As I've been saying, the sleep thinking program can have a question and answer format. You pose yourself questions about the issues that matter to you, and then, if and when the answers become available, you receive them. Answers arrive as direct information, in dreams, as feelings, as hunches, or in some other way, and they do so during the night, the next morning, or whenever else they happen to come to you.

But this is also only a part of the picture. For some people, just thinking will provide the answers to many of our problems, even our most pressing ones. But we rarely stop and think. As A. E. Houseman put it, with respect to a problem that could easily have been solved: "Three minutes thought would have sufficed to find this out; but thought is irksome and three minutes is a long time." Thought *is* irksome, and three minutes *does* feel like a long time. Why? Primarily because, as Albert Camus put it, "We get into the habit of living before we acquire the habit of thinking." Thinking is *a habit that many of us never fully acquire.* Even people with big brains are often not in the habit of thinking. Instead of just thinking about something important to us, we do other things, such as worrying, rushing to judgment, hazarding an opinion, using the opinions of experts, operating from a feeling, or employing some other second-rate method.

Even when we do think, we often do not "really" think. Just as there is careful cooking and careless cooking, cooking with fresh ingredients and cooking with stale ingredients, overcooking and undercooking, and so on, there is also careless thinking, thinking stale thoughts, over-thinking and under-thinking, and every other manner of "not-quite-right" thinking. As Brenda Ueland put it, "There are people who are always briskly doing something and are as busy as waltzing mice, and they have sharp little staccato ideas, such as 'I see where I can make an annual cut of $3.47 in my meat budget.' But they have no slow, big ideas." What Ueland is calling "slow, big ideas" I would like to call deep thinking. Working the sleep thinking program helps you become a regular thinker, which is rare enough, and also a deep thinker, which is even rarer.

Even when we fully intend to think something through, we can have significant trouble, mainly because our first thoughts on a subject often feel so trivial, confused, chaotic, boring, or incoherent that we quit after just a few seconds of trying. Marilyn vos Savant described it this way: "My thoughts are like waffles—the first few don't look too good." This is true for the majority of us. We stop ourselves from thinking because our first thoughts impress us so little that we see no good reason to continue.

It is for this reason that the sleep thinking program is organized in a question and answer format. It is easier to have deep thoughts when we formally ask ourselves questions. Just thinking should be enough and sometimes is enough, but the strategy of posing ourselves questions and endeavoring to answer them goes a long way toward making thinking a lifelong habit.

Since our first thoughts on a subject are often not our best ones and because we may not have acquired the habit of "just thinking" yet, a terrific question to ask ourselves with regard to *any* problem is, What are 20 possible solutions to this? As stated previously, by not having to dream up one "perfect" solution, you take the pressure off yourself and allow yourself the freedom to think deeply about your problem. Rather than say, What *should* I do?, you say, What are the 20 things I *might* do? Rather than say, What is *the* answer?, you say, What are *some* answers? This method allows for very big breakthroughs.

Take Kelly, a 33-year-old office manager. Kelly had just married Bob, a computer engineer six years her senior, after a whirlwind courtship. Suddenly, she found herself the stepmother of two young children, Lily, age 11, and Adam, age 9, and knew very quickly that she was in difficult straits. Bob believed that he had two wonderful children who, because of the trauma of the divorce, were experiencing some minor adjustment problems. From Kelly's point of view, Lily was a little witch, Adam was totally out of control, and they especially weren't very nice to her.

In order to survive her stepkids and save her marriage, Kelly posed herself the question, What are 20 things that would make my life better as a stepparent? Sitting at the kitchen table one Saturday morning while her husband drove the children to their soccer games, Kelly generated the following answers:

1. Get out.

2. Kill the kids.

3. Have my own child.

4. Let Bob deal with the kids.

5. Let Lydia (Bob's ex-wife) deal with the kids.

6. Bribe them.

7. Get a bigger house with two wings.

8. Sell them to the gypsies.

9. Forgive them. (For what exactly? For their attitude and behaviors? For just existing?)

10. Love them. (Don't know if I can.)

11. Let them teach me what to do. (Too painful?
Too dangerous?)

12. Order them around just because I can.

13. Read to them. (Would they laugh at me? Would they make me feel miserable?)

14. Never see them. Leave the room whenever they enter. (Very nice and loving!)

15. Cry.

16. Let them know what my rules are. (What are my rules?)

17. Soften. (Can't. Too dangerous. Don't want to. Then they'd be winning. Is this about winning and losing?)

18. Give it time. (Right. One more week will kill me.)

19. Talk to Bob. (But about what exactly? Just complain? Or something else?)

20. Whine and complain endlessly.

Kelly found many of her answers revealing and provocative. Most provocative was the idea of having a child as an answer to her current dilemma. Rationally, this made no sense. But intuitively, it seemed much less farfetched. Was that just wishful thinking on her part, supposing that a child of her own would improve her situation? Or was it that she just wanted a child, regardless of her circumstances?

That seemed to her to be the truth. She didn't have to sleep think on that or think about it at all. She did want a child.

But it made little sense to contemplate having a child when she found herself enmeshed in a situation that might even end in divorce. She did want a child, but that wasn't the answer.

However, it did serve as motivation. She found herself saying," I do want this to work out. I want to be with Bob and have a child with him. So I'd better start trying out some new things. Let me look at that list again." A couple of the answers on the list seemed obvious and true. She did need to cry, to grieve a little for this mess she'd gotten herself into. She did need to soften a little; staying hard as a rock, in order to protect herself, was fair neither to Bob nor the children, nor was it much of an answer. She also did need to love them—eventually. But what did she need to do right now? That she couldn't say.

She took that question to bed to sleep think: What should I do right now to make things a little better? A dream came to her in which she found herself a guest on a television show— she couldn't quite tell if it was a quiz show or a late-night talk show—and the host was asking her, "Okay, Kelly, what are the 20 small things you can do to make your life as a stepparent better? You know the rules, Kelly, start with number 20 first! Audience, a little encouragement!" After each answer, the host would say, "Okay, Kelly, is that your final answer?" And Kelly would think again and say, "Yes, that is my final answer." She got to her number 1 answer, and the dream ended abruptly. Kelly woke up, upset that she hadn't learned whether she'd won some grand prize. It was three in the morning. She got up and wrote down the list, as it had come to her in her sleep.

20. Get enough rest.

19. Yell if I have to.

18. Give hugs.

17. Buy an expensive sweater.

16. Be patient.

15. Say a nice thing to Bob.

14. Say a nice thing to Lily.

13. Say a nice thing to Adam.

12. Yell if I have to.

11. Be patient.

10. Make one rule that everybody is allowed to laugh about.

9. Yell if I have to.

8. Make one serious rule that nobody is allowed to laugh about.

7. Be patient.

6. Make popcorn for everybody.

5. Sew with Lily.

4. Sew with Adam.

3. Kiss Bob.

2. Be patient.

1. Yell if I have to.

She had to smile. She didn't imagine that her list had won her much of a prize. But it pleased her. It gave her some new ideas, some things that she thought she might try right out, and a sense of hopefulness for the first time in a long time. She realized that from the beginning she'd been pessimistic about this working out. When Bob told her that he had two children and that he was their primary caretaker, from that first instant she'd thought of Lily and Adam as problems. Now, at 3:30 in the morning, she had a glimpse of the possibility that maybe they were children, not problems.

Neither sleep thinking nor anything else will help you solve the problem of how to grow two feet taller so that you can play center in the NBA or how you can become a bass if you're currently a soprano. But there are so many types of problems that we are fully able to solve. And even if we can't solve a problem completely—just as Kelly couldn't completely resolve how to live with and mother her two stepchildren—a partial answer is better than no answer at all.

What Is a Problem? And Where Do Answers Come From?

We are always posing questions and trying to solve our problems, even if we have no conscious idea that we are doing so. We may not realize that we are upset with ourselves for giving our favorite sweater to our sister just because she asked for it, but then one day, we get the powerful urge to buy a new sweater, to make up for the loss. We may have no idea that we're annoyed with ourselves for contemplating retirement in the country, having forgotten how much the country bores us, until one day we wake up with the pressing need to research the possibility of retiring in London.

Our brain has noticed something, identified it as a problem, understands that we are upset about it, and has gone about arriving at a solution, all the while not bothering us with the matter. This is the sort of "multi-tasking" that our brain is expert at.

It goes on all the time. We may simultaneously be processing an insult we received last week, chiding ourselves that we weren't attentive enough during the last months of our dad's illness (even though he died a decade ago), and trying to figure out whether that tiny crack in our car windshield is worth worrying about. And the answer to *any* issue that our brain has been working on may come forward at any time.

Maybe a recent event triggered an association. Maybe our brain finally arrived at an answer that it's been seeking for months. Maybe the solution to one problem suggested a solution to another problem. Whatever the reason, we suddenly find ourselves presented with something—in a dream, as a bright idea—that seems to have come out of left field. We had no idea that we were even wrestling with that problem, let alone that we were on the verge of a solution. Then an answer arrives.

The following is a good example of what I mean. A therapist I know had no idea whatsoever that she was mulling over the question, Am I too prim? But then one night she had the following dream.

I dreamt that I was shopping for an old-fashioned dress and bonnet with a friend of mine. The dress was yellow with flowers. My friend, Robin, is a practicing Mormon, so shopping for an old-fashioned dress and bonnet with her made sense to me. But what was really strange and what puzzled me was that I was looking for gum to match.

At first I thought the gum meant I was trying to be a child again and that maybe the dress meant something about me hiding my sexuality. Then I realized that Robin has five children (pretty fertile).

As I was mulling over the gum part some more, I remembered that shortly before my father died, when I was 17, he asked me to stop chewing gum because it wasn't ladylike. After he died, I felt obligated to uphold my promise. I think shopping for the gum in my dream symbolized my attempt to retrieve the sassiness I toned down to please my father. I went right out and bought myself a pack of gum.

This is a good example of how the mind works "unconsciously." But this dream provides us with some other important information, too. Sometimes the "solution" to a "problem" is something as seemingly small as buying a pack of gum. You may never have considered that buying a pack of gum could possibly be a large answer to anything. But it can be. It can be a profound symbolic liberation. Making an important one-minute phone call that we've been putting off, taking a first step in a new direction, sending away for a college catalog, calling the information number for a career training course, or telling our lover in one clear sentence something that's been on our mind for years are "small, simple" actions full of meaning and can be the *complete* solution to even the most difficult of problems.

The demands of life can produce an endless stream of problems. We sometimes create our problems by the way we think about things and by the actions we take. Even the activities intended to give us a respite from our problems can themselves be problems, such as finding a vacation paradise that we can afford and that lives up to its brochure billing. In other words, to quote the first and most memorable line of Scott Peck's *The Road Less Traveled*, "Life is difficult."

Because life is difficult, we are always in flux. We are far from a solution to one problem, near to a solution to another problem, and finding a solution to yet another that affects everything else and completely reorders our inner landscape.

This is why the sleep thinking program can prove so valuable to you. It gives you a way to focus on one problem at a time and helps your brain know that while there are many problems it might concern itself with, there is one in particular that you'd like to give some special attention and consideration. Your brain will still go on working on additional problems, waking you up one morning with a dream that sends you out for a pack of gum. But it will also try to focus on the question you ask.

All of this is complicated enough. Then we come to the matter of the supernatural and the paranormal. Throughout this book, I've been describing sleep thinking as a profound but straightforward brain skill. You enlist your brain to solve your problems. No supernatural agencies or paranormal abilities have entered the picture, and I leave the question of whether any such agencies or abilities are involved in sleep phenomena to your personal belief system. No doubt you have some strong opinions about whether supernatural forces exist or whether everything can ultimately be explained scientifically.

But whatever your belief system, I think it would be a mistake to think of sleep—or life, for that matter—as unmysterious. Consider the report of a therapist of my acquaintance whose son died at the young age of 17. Of course, to call this death a "problem" that can be "solved" is a misuse of language. Yet tragedies *are* problems, and sleep can prove the best time to recover from them, to the extent that we can recover. I want to expand our definition of problem solving to include this woman's story and to acknowledge that sleep, whether or not it is populated by spirits, is certainly a time of mystery. It may even be a vehicle for healing.

I had this dream approximately 10 months after my 17-year-old son, Matthew, died. In the dream, we were at his best friend's party, at a place that looked like the Emporium on Main Street in Disneyland. I was looking at pins of butterflies, angels, and turtles when I realized that Matthew was beside me. I had only started wearing them after he died. Then a door opened—like those in the theaters in the round at Disneyland. I panicked because I couldn't see Matt and started running around screaming his name. Then I saw him, only this time he was transparent, as if in another dimension, and standing in the middle of Stonehenge. Our family had seen Stonehenge about five years before he died. He said, "I'm okay, Mom. I'm in the Runes, and I'll see you on December 13."

I woke up knowing that he had positively said r-u-n-e-s, but I didn't know what they were, and December 13, which was about six months away, had no meaning. About a week after the dream, I was reading a One Spirit book club brochure and noticed a page selling "Runes" (Celtic fortune-telling stones). I supposed that I had probably seen this before, but it hadn't stayed in my consciousness. Then about a month later, the miniseries *Merlin* was on TV. One scene showed a magician in the middle of Stonehenge throwing the Runes. For some reason, I mentioned this dream to one of Matt's friends. This wasn't one of his closest friends, and I'm not sure why I mentioned it. He said that it was strange because a month before Matt died, they had started playing with the Runes.

I originally thought that I might die on December 13 of some year and that that was what Matt was referring to. But then I thought he might have meant that he would come to me again in a dream on December 13. In fact, I did dream about him again very early in the morning of December 13.

It was another powerful dream. I used to ask him if he knew how much pleasure I got by just looking at him. He'd always say that he did. In this dream, we were standing at easels (both of us are interested in art). I stared at him for ages, and he just smiled at me with his distinct smile. Those two dreams were the only ones I've had in which he was 17. In every other dream, he's about 12, the age he was when he contracted the disease that killed him.

Have you chosen a problem or issue to work on yet? Maybe this is the right time to begin. Tonight, ask yourself, Is anything bothering me? or What would I like to change? Then spend a few minutes tomorrow morning with your journal or, if you haven't started a journal yet, with a few sheets of blank paper. Ask yourself the prompt question again and try to answer it. Write for several pages. Then read what you've written, give some thought to your ideas, and decide what, if anything, you'd like to do next. Your next step might be to continue the sleep thinking program in earnest. ((•))

Reducing Your Stress

Contemporary people face an array of stressors, a combination of age-old ones as well as modern ones, that produce unusual levels of stress in virtually everyone. Even people who are doing quite well materially are likely to be suffering from the consequences of stress in this tense, busy, fast-moving world of ours.

Since the mechanics of survival have gotten easier in developed countries, you'd think that people could reduce their stress simply by telling themselves how good they have it. But because each of us must face our own life and death issues as well as everyday concerns regarding relationships, jobs, and so on, we can't avoid stress, no matter how good we may otherwise have it.

Many people today are troubled by the question of whether they matter at all. Others have grave difficulties realizing their talents and abilities and feel misused or underused much of the time. Finally, there are our survival needs, which are everything from earning a living to maintaining our health. We may have it good, but we are still alive, and that's all it takes for stress to enter the picture.

No general discussion of this sort captures what it feels like to be constantly stressed. Too many people are busy all the time. They sleep poorly, are on the verge of feeling out of control, are beset by physical ailments that are partly stress related, are often unhappy about their career and relationship choices, feel pressured to keep up with technological change and a shifting landscape at work, and, on top of all of that, possess a psyche with its primitive side churning up bad dreams and strange obsessions.

If our career is boring, we get stressed. If our child is in trouble, we get stressed. Stress and anxiety are parts of the human condition, related to the body's perception of danger and its need to defend and protect itself. Sometimes our principles feel threatened, sometimes our self-image feels threatened, sometimes our physical well-being feels threatened, and sometimes our very meaning feels threatened.

Some stressors—floods, famines, the death of a child, war—are extremely powerful. *Cataclysmic stressors* of such magnitude will turn hair gray and devastate our lives. However, the scars may heal with time, and emotional recovery may come one day.

Then there are those stressors, the vast majority that we encounter, that are minor and that are experienced as stress because we inflate their importance and label them as threatening. This is the stress that we make for ourselves. Why should giving a small speech to one's peers feel so terribly stressful? Yet public speaking is the universal number one phobia. But speaking in public is only a stressor because our mind makes it one. It is a *contingent stressor*, that is, it is contingent on how we think about it.

Another class of stressors are those that arise because we aren't living our life in accordance with our sense of how life should be lived. This is *misalignment stress*, the stress caused when our life and our vision of life are not aligned. Correct alignment is a three-part affair: first, we need a vision of life that feels meaningful; second, the vision needs attainable goals (though the journey may be arduous and the odds long); and third, our life needs to align with and support that vision. If we do not have a meaningful vision, we experience stress. If we have a meaningful vision but can't reach our goals, we experience stress. If we have a meaningful vision but our life doesn't align with it, we experience stress.

Simplifying your life and modifying your thoughts are the two most frequently offered stress cures. Instead of commuting, you work from home. If that isn't possible, you take charge of your thoughts as you sit in your daily traffic jam and say to yourself, "I am fine and this will pass," instead of "I am wasting my life and I hate myself." Other stress reduction recommendations include getting more rest and exercise, learning how to relax, eating a good diet, and living a physically and mentally healthier life. These quite sensible cures can go a long way to reducing our experience of stress when that stress is contingent stress. But they can't really touch misalignment stress. In order to reduce misalignment stress, the only solution is *thinking*.

You can use sleep thinking to reduce contingent stress and even cataclysmic stress, but it is singularly valuable in the way it helps reduce misalignment stress. Sleep thinking helps you arrive at your vision. It helps you ascertain whether you can achieve your goals. It helps you gauge whether the life you're living supports your vision and, if it doesn't, identifies the changes you must make. Thus, you reduce your stress by living the life you ought to be living.

Sleep Thinking Stress Solutions

When Marvin came to see me he was a 50-year-old ex-lawyer who, the year before, had grown so sick of the legal life that he'd stopped practicing. Born into a musical family, with a sister who sang professionally and a brother who played violin in a symphony orchestra, Marvin had always wanted to compose. For the longest time, he'd had a symphony in mind, some of whose themes had been running through his head for 20 years. But he'd never learned the rudiments of symphonic composition, and his full law practice left him no time to honor his dream. Finally, at the end of his rope, he'd had a medium-sized breakdown.

Burned out, overworked, and deeply unhappy, he found himself unable to sleep, wracked with severe stomach pains and headaches, and on some days suicidal. In this state, unable to keep his clients' needs in mind and aware that he had to do something, he decided to leave his practice to study music composition. He had enough money saved so that he could live for a few years; beyond that he couldn't think. He just knew that not honoring his need to compose was killing him.

When he came to see me, he was in graduate school, trying to catch up on his musical education. Although he had taken a gigantic step toward aligning his life and felt much better since leaving his law practice, his stress level was still enormous, and he found himself completely blocked. He couldn't compose; he wasn't practicing the piano; and he was failing to meet the deadlines laid down by his graduate program. It looked as if he'd traded one crisis for another. It wasn't that he regretted leaving his law practice, but it saddened and dismayed him that he was having so much trouble trying to create. He wondered whether he still could compose or whether he'd waited too long to begin.

There were several things I did with him right from the start. First, I asked him to go easier on himself. Almost everyone is too self-critical and too guilt-ridden. This self-abuse weighs us down. This was certainly the case with Marvin. I also made it a point to praise him. I wanted him to truly recognize what a brave thing he'd done in giving up his law practice. I wanted him to understand that he'd taken a big risk but that he hadn't been reckless, especially since his life had been so out of alignment that he'd actually had no choice in the matter. He'd done the courageous thing of trying to save his life.

Still, he needed to make some important changes. He needed to affirm the importance of his daily piano practice and institute a good practice routine. He needed to substitute new positive thoughts for the ones about his worthlessness and past failures currently swirling in his head. He needed to find a composition teacher to supplement the conservatory staff, because he needed the additional help. There were many concrete things that Marvin needed to do to made this transition work. But the most important thing he had to do was consciously work on stress management.

I had him begin to sleep think the question, How can I find the calmness to compose? His anxiety level about being too old to produce anything of merit was clearly interfering with his ability to create. Lowering that anxiety level was a top priority. The next session he came back with a list. Many ideas had come to mind. First, he felt he needed to do a better job of keeping up with his religious practice, which, when he remembered to give it time, always comforted and calmed him. Second, he needed to stop smoking marijuana, which he'd started smoking with some of his new musician friends after years of not imbibing. The marijuana was the wrong way to feel arty and the wrong way to reduce his stress. Third, he needed to swim. Swimming had always worked to reduce his stress, and he saw that however awkward it was to fit swimming into his schedule, he had to find a way.

For the next week, I had Marvin sleep think the question, And? By this I meant, And what else is needed in my life to help me calm down, compose, and succeed? I had the impression that the list Marvin created was still missing some essential elements, ones that addressed the residual misalignment issues in his life. Marvin's current life didn't support his goals well enough. For instance, he'd start the day with religious meditation, which seemed appropriate, but then he'd read the morning newspaper for an hour, which seemed inappropriate. So I asked Marvin to think about these matters and to sleep think the question, And?

He returned the next week with an insight. He read the newspaper every morning because he was afraid to compose and afraid even to approach the piano in his apartment. In response to the question And? he'd gotten the clear, unambiguous message that he had to institute a routine and follow that routine to the letter, because his own fears were preventing him from making progress. In session, we worked out the details of that routine, including which warm-up fingering exercises he would use and how long he would warm up, how long he would spend at the piano before permitting himself his first break, and so on.

I ended the session asking him to again sleep think the question, And? The next week he came in noticeably more relaxed. He said that nothing new had come to him and that he had the sense that nothing else was needed. He simply had to do what he now knew to do. He had to commit to his composing in a way that was at once simple and deep; sticking to his routine would be proof of that commitment. He had to use all of the stress management tools at his disposal, from prayer to swimming, and he had to balance two contradictory ideas, that he take it easy but that he work hard. He felt that for the first time, he was squarely on his own path.

Today, Marvin is composing classical songs, some of which have been performed and critically well-received. He has many composing projects in mind and manages to complete work on a regular basis. As a poorly paid composer, he's necessarily living hand to mouth, giving lessons, accompanying singers, and doing a variety of things in and about the world of music. To make ends meet, he is also seeing a few law clients; he helps struggling musicians with their contracts, their disputes with club owners and managers, and other music-related legal problems.

Of course, this was a source of concern to us. It wasn't at all clear that even a small amount of legal work would align with his new life. We watched to see if his stress level would skyrocket. I also made him aware that since it was easier to see clients than to sit in front of the piano, it was altogether possible that he might build up his practice and end up misaligned and stressed out all over again. It was a paradox that he understood well: He could make money and have an "easier" life as a lawyer, but he had to choose the harder path in order stay in self-alignment. Only the harder path would serve him.

Helping Cure Stress-Related Illnesses

Nicole's case was different. As a young woman, she'd translated her love of horses and her flair for adventure into a rodeo career that lasted almost 10 years. She did well and even won her event at some small rodeos. But after too many broken bones, too many stress-related ailments, and too much poverty, she found herself unable to sustain the rodeo life. At that point, she started working for a small manufacturing company in rural California, first as a secretary and later as the office manager.

Her new job wasn't a mismatch, even though it didn't connect to her love of horses or her love of the outdoors. It challenged her and interested her, and just as she'd thrown herself into the rodeo life, Nicole now threw herself into her job. She took on more and more responsibilities and worked longer and longer hours. The same stress-related illnesses she'd had to deal with on the rodeo circuit returned with a vengeance, but even her illnesses didn't slow her down. The company owners promoted her over employees senior to her and went so far as to tell her that the business would fall apart without her heroic efforts. That flattery caused her to redouble her efforts.

Nicole had married young, while still on the rodeo circuit, but got divorced a few years later. She dated after that but never remarried. She began to sense that children and a second marriage weren't in the cards and started spending her free time with her sister and her sister's children, a boy and two girls. As it does for all of us, time flew by, and suddenly Nicole was approaching 50. On her 50th birthday she received an odd and very extravagant present from her eldest niece; it was a complete oil painting set-up that included an easel, paints, thinner, brushes, canvases, and even an assortment of palette knives. Nicole couldn't have been more surprised, but her niece laughingly told her she'd had a vision of Nicole painting; she'd honored that vision by buying all these supplies.

For a full year, the painting supplies remained unused. Nicole hid them away, took them out, and hid them away again. She felt too untalented and too much of a beginner even to try to paint. It occurred to her to take a class at the nearby junior college, and each semester she got the school's catalog but never enrolled. She told herself that she didn't have any time to take a class because she worked late on most nights and had to get her chores done on the weekend. But she knew deep down that she was just too scared to begin.

Then one of her stress-related illnesses hit. The shingles-like viral attack was the worst she'd ever experienced, and the pain was just about unbearable. With it came a bad case of the flu, a high fever, and terrible headaches. Instead of losing a few days of work, as had happened in the past, Nicole found herself in bed for two weeks. Finally, the fever broke. To her surprise, when she awoke on the first morning that she felt well, she heard herself clearly say, "I've got to paint."

She screwed up her courage and enrolled at the junior college. Her first drawing class astounded her. She saw her drawings improve dramatically over the course of just a few weeks and realized that good drawing had little to do with talent and much more to do with relaxing and using her eyes. She discovered that when she drew, time stood still. She could feel her anxieties slip away and her self-confidence build as she spent time enjoying nature with her fellow drawing students.

For years, she'd imagined that she should volunteer her time at a hospice or a retirement home and that that was the way to use her spare time and edge into retirement. But now she understood that for her own mental health and well being, she needed a meditative practice such as drawing and not a volunteer job. In her own heart she knew that she would overdo a volunteer job and lose herself again, just as she always had lost herself at work. The practice of art was a way to find herself. When the first basic drawing class ended, she took a second class, live model drawing, and then her first painting class.

Then one Sunday, after she'd been taking classes for more than a year, it occurred to her to go into the country and sketch horses. She found a busy riding stable, sat on an old log, and drew for hours. Ranch dogs came up and sniffed her, trail riders rode by, cars came and went, dropping off and picking up young riders. Nicole felt blissful. That afternoon marked the beginning of her life as a Western painter.

The long stock market advance had produced a healthy retirement nest egg for Nicole, and she realized that she could retire at 60. Previously, the thought of retirement hadn't attracted her in the slightest, and she'd even thought that she might work until she was physically unable to continue. But the more she pursued her art, spending a day each weekend sketching outdoors and a day indoors painting, the more she longed for retirement. She began to plan for the day when she would retire from work, and when that day arrived, she felt nothing but jubilation.

Now Nicole paints Western scenes. She had no idea that she would love drawing and painting so much, but she does. She purchased a four-wheel-drive vehicle and takes long trips to the Nevada desert, near Virginia City, where wild mustangs still run. Often she goes with the same niece who presented her with that first painting kit. They laugh a lot about Nicole's path from rodeo cowgirl to Western painter, they camp out, and they even sing old cowboy songs. Nicole's stress-related ailments rarely return, and she's never felt better.

Nicole had never really been out of alignment. Her job had served her, and she hadn't battled it internally. But her personality was such that she couldn't relax. She had never relaxed, which made her an ideal worker, but it robbed her of the opportunity to open her heart and quiet her nerves. Exercise was not going to do the trick; she exercised plenty. She ate well, had good friends, and didn't beat herself up with negative self-talk. But she didn't have a way to channel her intensity. The phrase *I've got to paint* which came to her as her feverish state ended and her brain cleared, was really an answer to a question that Nicole didn't know she was posing herself: Given that I create stress for myself by virtue of my personality, what is my best path?

Marvin engaged in some formal sleep thinking in order to address the stress in his life. Nicole didn't. But from the moment she received those painting supplies from her niece, important inner questioning began, for the most part out of conscious awareness and during her sleep. She knew that the painting supplies were meaningful, which is why it disturbed her so much not to be making use of them. But she couldn't tell why they were meaningful until, as the culmination of a long informal sleep thinking process, she let herself know that only something like painting could save her life.

Bringing Up Anxiety

A client in psychotherapy once said to me, "You shouldn't bring up anxiety in the first session. It makes a person feel too anxious!" Most therapists understand this perfectly and make it their business not to talk directly about anxiety. They fear upsetting (and losing) their clients. But I find it too important too avoid. Therefore, I look for it behind clients' reports and always find it, not because I'm inventing it but because it's always there. I have never met a nonanxious person, and I don't believe that one exists.

A low-grade anxiety is always present in the human animal. You are forced to say yes and no hundreds of times a day, and every single choice point is a small anxiety moment. You have to decide whether to purchase this blouse or that one. You have to choose between the Cheerios and the Rice Krispies. And while these are the easiest decisions in life, even they make us a little queasy. Isn't shopping for slacks strangely stressful? Isn't supermarket shopping a small trial? Can't even choosing what show to watch on TV feel like a monumental task? Even these inconsequential decisions make us anxious, perhaps because every decision forces us to confront the daunting question, How should I be living my life?

Unless anxiety has caught us in its grip so severely that we're paralyzed, we manage to say yes and no in these small matters fairly easily. We manage to pick between the cranapple juice and the cranraspberry. But when we perceive that the decision is important, we get considerably more anxious. If the blouse we've gone out to buy is for a major business presenta-tion, then whether it should be a creamy beige or a whiter white suddenly matters tremendously. As soon as we perceive a matter as important, anxiety bites us.

Most people try to deny that life makes them anxious. But their denial does very little to prevent them from experiencing the anxiety. Sometimes they experience it directly, as phobic reactions, panic attacks, butterflies in the stomach, sudden urges to urinate, and so on. More often they experience it indirectly, as indecisiveness, procrastination, mental confusion, lightheadedness, fatigue, depression, addictions, or insomnia. Their denial doesn't serve the intended purpose of helping them lead a happy, productive life. It only produces a multitude of ailments and keeps them from knowing what's really going on inside their own being.

Even the person who seems to admit that he's anxious often isn't making a real admission. He may admit that playing the violin in public makes him nervous and that that's why he's abandoning his dreams of a solo career. But what he's saying may not amount to a true confession. If you ask, "Why don't you try some relaxation techniques or maybe a breathing exercise or two?" he won't have an answer. He'll probably make some kind of offhand gesture and say, "They don't work for me," or "I'm too anxious to try." He won't have an answer because he isn't really ready to admit to being anxious. That admission would make him feel *too* anxious! He is abandoning the violin not because playing it in public makes him too anxious, but because thinking about his anxiety makes him too anxious.

Nonadmission admissions of this sort are like an addict's dodge. The addict says, "Sure, I'm addicted," just to end the discussion. But he isn't admitting that he's addicted. He isn't really admitting that he's anxious and powerless and ruining people's lives. If you say to him, "I hear that treatment program in the valley is really terrific and might help you break your addiction," he'd probably just get angry.

"What? Are you calling me an addict?" he'll retort.

"But *you* called yourself an addict."

"Sure, sure, but that was *different*!"

It was different. You meant it. He didn't.

Our mind works this way. It allows us to say, "Maybe I'm an addict, but, then again, maybe I'm not." When it's convenient for us to think of ourselves as addicted, we're free to think that. When it's more convenient to think of ourselves as not addicted, we're free to think that, too. Sounds like a pretty convenient solution, but, of course, it isn't. It's just a lie with bad consequences. The addict who manages to escape this trap and can bear his own anxiety is able to say, "I can't drink. Sorry." He can say, "I'm feeling really anxious, and that's why I'm thinking about hanging out with my buddies. That's where the dope is." He isn't less anxious than before or more anxious than before. What he's managed to do is tear down the wall that used to keep his anxiety hidden from his own eyes. Now he can see the truth, which can set him free.

Many interesting psychological experiments have been conducted that demonstrate the negative effects caused by our unwillingness to look at and ventilate our feelings of anxiety. In an elegantly simple experiment, subjects were shown a pair of lines, one of which was obviously longer than the other. When a subject was shown the two lines in the absence of any pressure, he told the truth and said that the lines were of unequal length. But if you put him in a room with confederates of the experimenter and had those confederates assert that the two lines were of equal length, the subject crumbled. Suddenly, he felt compelled to lie and say that the lines were of equal length. Instead of recognizing that the testimony of his peers filled him with anxiety and that in order to stick to his guns he would have to experience even more anxiety, he lied. This is how peer pressure works and beautifully demonstrates the power of unacknowledged anxiety.

Consider another experiment. You're shown a painting. You like it. You say that you like it. Then the person next to you says that she doesn't like it. What happens? A person who lacks insight about the presence and power of anxiety in such situations is likely to change his mind. Internally, he's going to say, "Maybe I was wrong to like it," "Maybe I don't know how to judge a painting," or "Maybe that gal's right. She looks intelligent." When you ask the subject of this experiment a second time whether or not he likes the painting, he's going to tell you that now he likes it a lot less. In the actual experiments, researchers found that *all* subjects confronted by antagonistic views yielded considerably in their stated preferences. This suggests that all of us are liable to fail ourselves when we don't know to what extent anxiety is affecting us.

Anxiety isn't the problem. The problem is our ignorance about the central place of anxiety in our life. If you learn about anxiety and the way it manifests itself in your life, you'll have acquired the most important education of all. When the person in front of you, who really must know that she's going to have to pay for her groceries, acts surprised when the clerk holds out his hand for money, you'll realize that her fumbling with her purse, her mumbled apologies, and her attempts at finding the exact change are manifestations of her ignorance about her own anxious nature. All you need to say in order to explain the situation to yourself is, "Wow, anxiety is everywhere!"

If you begin to understand your behavior— and human behavior in general—in terms of the underlying anxiety, you'll become observant and wise. You'll start to understand things that used to perplex you and make you mad. Maybe you've been perplexed by the fact that your mate can't tell the truth.

Now you can name the problem accurately. The idea of telling the truth just fills him with too much anxiety. The *idea* fills him with too much anxiety. Telling the truth might serve him well; experience suggests that telling the truth is often a positive, liberating experience. But when he thinks about telling the truth, he experiences vast anxiety. He gets a warning signal from his miswired mind, and inside he gets the wordless message, "The truth will kill you, man!" So he lies.

Stress reduction and anxiety intuition are partners. The more you understand the place of anxiety in human affairs, the less stressful you'll find all situations. This is also the most important area of life to which you should devote a little sleep thinking time. You might try any of the following as sleep thinking prompts:

》 Do I have an anxious nature?
》 Do I have an *especially* anxious nature?
》 Which of my behaviors are rooted in anxiety?
》 Am I brave enough to look anxiety in the eye?
》 Which of my dreams for the future are stalled because of my anxiety?
》 What am I prevented from doing because of anxiety?
》 Do I know when I'm anxious?
》 What are the telltale signs of my anxiety?
》 What do I need to know about my anxiety?

The goal of sleep thinking anxiety questions is not to eliminate anxiety (though that may result) but to move from anxiety ignorance to anxiety understanding. You want your own brain to know that it has permission to notice anxiety, to think about it, to confront it, to embrace it, and to provide you with a real anxiety education. Tell it that it has that permission by inviting it to sleep think about the role of anxiety in your life. You may get anxiety dreams, nightmares, and strange information that's hard to interpret. But you'll also get an education.

Singing For Fun and Meaning

Edith, a singer, came to see me with many things on her mind. Front and center was her sense that she was too anxious much of the time. Although an accomplished singer, she hated listening to tapes of her concerts because she could hear nothing but her errors. She had the desire to try to teach a class in Renaissance music at the local junior college, but her fears got in the way of her proposing it. The week-long visits that her mother-in-law made three times a year drove her almost out of her skin. Her recent move from a diverse urban community to a snobbish enclave in the California wine country further upset and disturbed her. She wasn't sure that she liked the values of her new neighbors or that she would fit in, and such thoughts made her feel lonely and more anxious.

When so many things are going on, it's hard to know what to focus on. You may find identifying a starting point the hardest part of your sleep thinking program. But if you already know that many things are making you anxious, you can always start with the prompt, What is *really* making me anxious? or What is the *biggest* stressor in my life? You can use that as your initial sleep thinking question and assume that a door will open through which you can move in the appropriate direction. Edith identified her mother-in-law's visits as her biggest stressor, probably because a visit was approaching. In my own mind, I doubted whether this could be the central issue in Edith's life, but there was no reason not to begin there.

She took the question, What can I do about my mother-in-law's visit? to bed to sleep think. The answer came to her within a few nights: Tell my husband to tell her not to come. In session, she told me that she couldn't bring it up to her husband. Kurt felt very responsible toward his mother and wouldn't hear of upsetting or offending her by telling her not to come. I asked Edith whether she was sure about that, and she said that she was. I then asked her if she would ask Kurt anyway, since his mother's visits were so stressful that they might harm her ability to perform her holiday concerts. We role-played what Edith might try saying and how Kurt might reply. She left agreeing that she would at least bring up the matter.

To her complete surprise, Kurt agreed with her request, saying that he had lots of work to do over the holidays and that his mother could wait until the spring to visit. Feeling almost giddy, Edith wondered aloud whether they might take a short vacation together over the holidays, even just a long weekend away. Kurt agreed to this, too. In no time, they'd picked out a vacation getaway package and were even laughing about how Kurt's mother was going to take the news that she'd been disinvited.

This success gave her hope. In the next session I asked her what she wanted to focus on next. She replied instantly, "the music." I asked her whether she wanted to focus on her inability to take joy in performing, her desire to stretch into teaching, or something else. She shook her head and said that she didn't know. I asked her whether she could frame a sleep thinking question with respect to the music. She thought about that and then opened the pad on her lap and began writing. She wrote for a while, looked up, and said, "It's not a question, it's a paragraph."

She read me the paragraph:

I am an anxious person. I get down on myself. I sing serious music very seriously. I hate what's called music today. I don't fit into this time or place. I hate it when people look bored by what I sing. I hate it that I have so few opportunities to sing. I wish—something. I don't know what. Does life make me anxious, or do I make life anxious? I need to change—a lot. But what? It's about me, but it's also about the music. But what?

I said, "Just read the whole paragraph to yourself before you go to sleep and see what happens." She agreed. When she came in for her next session, she announced that she'd had a week that started out very hard but that ended excellently. She had read herself the paragraph before going to bed that first night and awakened the next morning with a clear message: "Sing for fun." But she found that phrase extraordinarily disturbing. She'd sat with her journal, not writing, just thinking. "Sing for fun." The phrase made her very sad.

At first she thought that to have so much trouble enjoying what she loved doing seemed pathetic and must be what was making her sad. But very quickly she realized that the problem was something else. The problem wasn't that she couldn't have fun singing, though it was true that singing often felt more like torture than work. The bigger problem was that "sing for fun" didn't really sound meaningful to her own ears. Later that day, she heard herself exclaim, "I can't sing for fun. Fun is trivial!"

For days the phrases "sing for fun" and "fun is trivial!" kept going through her brain. Then one night a new sleep thinking question popped into her head: If fun is trivial, what *is* important?

No answer came to her, but as she sat with her journal the next morning, she found herself making a list in response to that question. On the list she put:

Paying bills? No!

Shopping and cooking? No!

Cleaning? No!

Earning my own money? Don't know. Maybe.

Spending time with Kurt? Yes. In a way. But . . .

Having children? Don't know. Maybe.

Writing, painting, something like that? Don't know.

Good causes? Sure. But . . .

All kinds of music? Don't know. Close to yes.

Classical music? Yes, but.

An idea was on the tip of her tongue. It had something to do with life meaning, but she couldn't corral it, not then, or later that day, or during the night. The next day she had a very bad day. She couldn't practice, she couldn't pay the bills, she couldn't even put together the soup she'd intended to make. She knew that she was depressed, and early in the afternoon, she dragged herself off for a nap. As she slept, words and phrases kept cycling and recycling through her mind: *Serious. Serious music. Classical music. Seriousness. Music. Musical. Deadly serious. Deathly serious. Music. Musical.* She woke up with the word *music* on her lips. Then a question came to her that seemed like a variation of some previous question but that also felt different. It was, If music isn't important, what is?

The next day she woke up almost jubilant. Some time during the night she'd made the decision to treat herself to an all-day visit to her favorite music store. It had lots of world and classical music and a wide variety of CDs to sample in every section, and you could sit, put on earphones, and listen to as much or as little of hundreds of CDs as you liked. She got there almost as soon as the store opened and, rejoicing in the variety of titles available to her, spent the next four hours listening to music from all over the world, in every style, from every era. When she took a coffee break at a nearby café, she heard herself say, "If music isn't important, what is?"

At first it seemed like a rhetorical question. Of course, music was important. But then she saw that it was a real question and that she had to address it. Was music more important than everything else? Was she supposed to devote her life to it, turning herself over to it as if she were a disciple of a religion? Before she could answer that question, she had another thought: "Meaning can't be made in just one way." This struck her as a great insight. She suddenly realized that singing her classical songs was too narrow an endeavor. It wasn't that she needed to have "more fun" with her singing; it was that she had to take music much more seriously by teaching it, learning more about it, expanding her horizons, giving more concerts, searching out more opportunities, and letting go of self-criticism.

She could feel herself moving toward something she heard herself calling "integration." She also felt calmer than she had in years, even though she was setting herself up for more stress, in the way of more concerts, more studying, a new life of teaching, and so on. She saw that her goal couldn't be to "simplify," except in the sense that life became simple when you knew what you wanted to do. Still, she felt ready and to seal the deal with herself, she returned to the music store and listened to another three hours of music, including things she never in her life would have called "real music."

Sometimes you can reduce your stress and anxiety by trying out a relaxation tape, a breathing exercise, or some new thoughts. But often deeper work has to go on, the work of alignment, in which you bring your existence into alignment with your beliefs and your dreams. When life feels meaningful, then your stress level goes down—even if your life is very hard. When life feels misaligned, then your stress level goes up—even if your life is easy. If you use the sleep thinking program to accomplish this alignment work, you can reduce your stress dramatically.

((·))

Upgrading Your Personality

One of the things you may want to do is upgrade your personality. If that's a goal of yours, sleep thinking can be of great help. But altering personality can be exceedingly difficult. Take the case of Mike, a young guitarist who couldn't make himself solo.

Mike was 20 years old, attended a community college, and played in a small band after school and on the weekends. He loved playing, and the band was becoming quite good, lining up small gigs around their home town, gaining a small following, and even beginning to write their own music. But Mike was plagued by his inability to solo. He couldn't make himself solo at gigs, and he couldn't even solo at rehearsals, even though at home, when he was alone, he could play lightning-quick, breathtaking riffs without error.

In front of the other band members—the drummer, bassist, and lead singer—he felt paralyzed. Whenever he tried to step out in front and take a solo during rehearsals, which the lead singer often invited him to do, he froze up and had to shake his head. Nobody in the band questioned him about his reluctance, and for his part, he shrugged the matter off with wisecracks such as, "I'll solo when I get my neon-green Jimi Hendrix outfit!"

For months he tried to figure out what was going on, but he couldn't make sense of it. It didn't feel like stage fright, or what he imagined stage fright felt like. He didn't feel nervous at all at those moments. Nor did he doubt himself; he was positive that he could do it. What happened, as best as he understood it, was that the second he thought about soloing, he entered a state of slow motion, almost of suspended animation. The music, his playing, everything slowed down. When that occurred, he'd say to himself, "Damn, I can't solo with my fingers moving this slowly!" Then he'd wave the opportunity away, and instantly everything would return to normal.

After about six months of this, Mike decided to try sleep thinking. First he compiled a list of possible sleep thinking questions.

» Why can't I solo in front of the band?
» Am I nervous or is it something else?
» Am I meant to be a guitar player?
» What would the band think if I did solo?
» How can I make myself solo?

Mike choose to sleep think a variation of the first question: Why can't I solo, even just in front of the band? He hoped that a question that direct would help focus and free his mind to really think about the problem. That very night he dreamed that Eric Clapton was in his band. Mike was able to solo this time, but after he did, Clapton came up to him and said, "Hey kid, I think you can do a lot better." Immediately the other band members started to boo Mike and shout, "Get off the stage, you turkey!"

Mike woke from this dream feeling hurt and dejected. He recorded the dream but tried not to think about it, because thinking about it made him furious with the band members. Who were they to boo him? He had to remind himself that it was only a dream, that nobody had actually booed him, and that his best bet was to forget about it. But he couldn't, because every night the exact same dream returned. Finally, he knew that he was going to have to think about what the dream was saying. As soon as he tried to interpret the dream, it occurred to him that the problem might center around the crazy idea that in order to solo he had to play as well as Eric Clapton. Was that what he was secretly thinking? Had he set himself up against that kind of ideal? Or was he worried that if he didn't play as well as Clapton, the band members would criticize him, either to his face or among themselves?

He knew that he had to figure out whether the problem was that he'd set too high a standard for himself or whether he feared what the others would say if he didn't amaze them with his soloing. Thinking about it, he concluded that the problem had to do with his own standards. So he decided to sleep think a new question: How can I not worry about "standards" and just solo? But the question framed that way didn't produce any results. Days and then weeks went by, and Mike found himself getting nowhere. He was still playing in the band and still avoiding taking any solos. As usual, nobody else in the band seemed to mind, because he continued to hold up his end. But he really wished that he could show them what he was capable of doing on the guitar.

As their next big gig approached, Mike decided to give up sleep thinking his last question. He'd just stop thinking about soloing. The decision saddened him, but he was tired of putting that pressure on himself. Then, at the last minute, he thought about the matter one last time. The members of his band certainly didn't intimidate him. Then it hit him. Maybe *Clapton* was intimidating him. But how could somebody who didn't know him, who wasn't there, and who would never hear him play be an intimidating figure? It made no sense, and yet it felt like the truth.

He saw that the problem was in himself, but in a way that he hadn't understood before. Yes, he had high expectations for himself. But he had no idea that he'd created a whole host of inner critics—including Hendrix and Clapton—who were intimidating him and preventing him from soloing. It was like something from a nightmare or a horror movie, this chorus of guitar greats laughing among themselves at his playing and hooting at every less than spectacular riff that he played.

Mike understood that he needed to change his personality and that he had arrived at a starting point, not an end point. He further understood that he had to transform himself into a more confident person, into someone who could play before the Claptons of the world—that is, before his severest critics—even if they were critics he himself had invented.

Many people get to this starting point and courageously identify that the problem they're having is with their own character. But then they don't know how to proceed. It isn't that they lack the will or the courage to go the next step. More often the problem is that they don't know what the next step should be. What do you think Mike should do? What would you suggest? Would it work to tell him, "Hey, man, just stop worrying!"? Would you offer him a quart of Scotch, nudge him in the ribs, and whisper, "Here, this'll boost your confidence!" Because personality change is as hard to *think about* as it is to do, most of us turn to bad remedies or throw up our hands and just give up.

Thinking About Personality Change

It's surprisingly hard to think about personality. The very fact that it is so hard to think about is one of the reasons why we balk at trying to make personality changes. We simply shake our head and say, "No way."

It's far easier to contemplate personality change if we think in terms of *personality traits* and not *personality*. Consider the following analogy. Somebody puts a loaf of bread in front of you and says, "Make another loaf, only better." You'd go, "Duh?" You wouldn't know what was wanted or where to begin. But if you were told, "This bread is too salty; the next loaf should have half the salt" or "This bread is too glutinous; the next loaf should be kneaded for about half the time," you'd have a clear sense of what was wanted.

The same is true about personality. If I were to say to Mike, "Remake yourself into a better person," he wouldn't know where to begin. But if I said to him, "Let's work on your confidence. A person who is confident takes certain kinds of risks. Let's try this out for homework: The next time your band rehearses, I want you to step forward and do a brief solo. You aren't trying to sound good; how you sound doesn't matter. You might think that it does matter and that if you don't sound good, you'll be embarrassed and won't want to solo again. But that's not the way we're going to think about it. You're going to say to yourself, 'Eventually my soloing will sound great, but right now I am soloing *just to become a better risk taker*. I understand that risk taking and building confidence go hand in hand."

One of the great secrets about personality change is that when you work on *any* personality trait you change your *whole* personality in the process. And you have many choices, or many starting points, because there are a vast number of personality traits. (In connection with increasing creativity I've identified 75 important traits and written about them in *The Creativity Book* and *Living the Writer's Life.*)

Any adjective that you can think of that refers to human beings—assertive, cold, undisciplined, happy, silly, rude, self-confident, arrogant, boisterous, charming, loving, rebellious, self-trusting, thoughtful, and so on—represents a way to look at personality and can be singled out and called a personality trait. And any of these traits can be worked on to either develop or eliminate it.

Consider the following list of desirable personality traits.

1. Self-direction

2. Passion

3. Thoughtfulness

4. Confidence

5. Persistence

6. Empathy

7. Flexibility

8. Sense of humor

9. Discipline

10. Resiliency

11. Honesty

12. Assertiveness

13. Curiosity

14. Compassion

15. Self-Trust

16. Courage

17. Patience

18. Integrity

19. Awareness

20. Energy

Choose one trait from this list to sleep think. Your sleep thinking question might be, for example, Am I confident enough? or How does my lack of confidence affect me? or What can I do to increase my confidence level? It's likely that all 20 of these traits will strike you as valuable, but even if that's true and choosing is difficult, try to select the one that feels the most important for you to consider. If no single trait leaps out at you, try the following question as a sleep thinking prompt: If I wanted to change one thing about my personality, what would that be?

If you work directly on any one of these traits—whether it's self-confidence, compassion, patience, or any of the others—you'll be better equipped to solve your problems and reduce your stress. You'll also become a more creative person, since these traits are exactly the traits needed to maintain personal creativity.

Most of us aren't motivated or inclined to change. Often we just throw in the towel at the idea of change and say, even if we're quite young, "You can't teach an old dog new tricks." It turns out that it takes more courage to change than to brave machine-gun fire. I know, because I found it *much* easier to crawl under machine-gun fire as a soldier than to give up smoking or to really listen when people talked. It may be that personality change is hard because our defenses get in the way, because of some powerful unconscious desire in each of us not to change, because too much anxiety wells up when we contemplate change, or for a host of other reasons. We could make a very long list to explain what we already know: that personality change is hard.

But maybe you want to be one of those rare people who do grow and change. If so, try sleep thinking. You can work on upgrading your personality in the safety and sanctity of your own bed, wrapped in your favorite blanket, with the house quiet and your defenses disarmed. You might even wake up a changed person, for although personality change is both hard and rare, miracles of transformation do occur in an instant.

Q. *I'm not sure if I'm sleep thinking material. Are there some people who are not suited to do this sort of thing?*

Many people put obstacles in the way of their own sleep thinking, and there's evidence that some people, like severely depressed individuals and schizophrenics, are lacking in NREM sleep, which suggests that mental illness may reduce a person's ability to sleep think. But the general rule is that each of us is sleep thinking material. People of various cultures throughout history have used some version of sleep thinking to solve problems and plan for the future. We've just forgotten how to make the most of our brain potential at night.

If you're afraid of the answers you might receive—about what they would say about you or what work they would entail—you won't be very motivated to sleep think. If you're wishing for answers that run counter to the truth—if you're looking for some way not to be homosexual when you simply are, or hoping that your husband isn't having an affair when he simply is—you can have a very difficult and unrewarding sleep thinking experience. The chief obstacles to sleep thinking lie in human nature.

But the reason you may be wondering whether you're good sleep thinking material is that instead of waking up in the middle of the night with an "Aha!" experience, you may be waking up in the morning having answered some question or resolved some issue without any fanfare. You may have no sense that the process is working even though it is working extremely well. The chances are excellent that you're getting benefits even if you can't point to them directly.

Twelve Tips for Upgrading Your Personality

1. *Be able to say how you want to change. Here are some examples:*

    )) I want to do a better job of accepting myself.

    )) I need to stop drinking. Period.

    )) I get too anxious and obsessed about trivial things. I want to be able to look at some everyday problem, like my car's tires being underinflated or the kitchen grout looking filthy, and not ruin my day over it. Either I'll clean the grout or I won't, but I won't make myself miserable and get into a grand funk over it.

    )) I need either to accept others or ignore them. I'm tired of getting into a rage over the actions of people I see on television or at the grocery store. I need to find a way to become philosophical about human shortcomings and human nature.

    )) I need to do something about my critical nature. How does it help me to approach everything with a critical eye, as if I were the quality assurance inspector for the whole universe?

2. *Tell another person what change you are hoping to make. Here are some examples:*

    )) Send your brother an e-mail, telling him that you are working on becoming more communicative.

》 Announce to your eldest daughter that you are becoming a nonconformist and that she should go out and buy you a beret and temporary tattoos.

》 Tell your mate that you are transforming yourself into a more loving person and that she should expect lots of hugs and kisses from now on.

》 Tell your parents that they have to ask before they come visit for a week, because when they just show up without asking that forces you to put your life on hold.

》 Tell your boss that you want to open up a European branch of the company, because you're looking to stretch and take on some big challenges this year.

3. *Make a list of sleep thinking prompts, each one a little different from the next, aimed at a particular personality change. Then try them out on successive nights. Here is a sample set of prompts:*

》 What would make me more resilient?

》 How can I bounce back faster from life's blows?

》 Why do I stay down so long whenever something disturbing happens?

》 I was more resilient when I was younger. What happened?

》 What would put a spring into my step?

4. *Include a special reminder about personality change in your bedtime ritual. Here are some possibilities:*

》 While the water is coming to a boil for your bedtime cup of tea, remind yourself that you mean to become more self-trusting.

» As you brush your teeth, repeat your current affirmation; for example, say, "I am strong and assertive."

» When you light your bedtime candle, make a wish; for example, say, "I hope I can become the passionate person I'm dreaming of becoming."

» As you crawl into bed, wonder aloud, "What personality change should I think about tonight?"

» Add a personality change prompt to your current sleep thinking question. For example, say "I want to communicate better with Janice, but is the problem in her or in me?"

5. *Pick up a book on personality typology and see whether the idea of personality types is a congenial one. If you encounter a description that sounds like you, translate what you learn into sleep thinking questions. Here are some possibilities:*

» If Jungian typology interests you and you discover that you're an introverted type, ask yourself this question: What would it be like if I were more extroverted? Would that be useful?

» If, in reading Freud, it strikes you that you might be an anal type, ask yourself this question: How can I loosen up?

» If you happen upon Erikson and realize that you're basically mistrustful, ask yourself this question: Would it benefit me to be more trusting? Should I be a lot more trusting or just a little?

» If you like astrology, ask yourself this question: What do other signs manifest that mine doesn't? Can I add some of their good qualities to my basic nature?

》 Simply ask yourself the question: What is my personality type? or What is my basic nature? or Who am I?

6. *Imagine something that you would love to do but that you
don't think yourself capable of doing. Try to identify the personality change that would be required in order for you to
realize your dream and turn that insight into a sleep thinking
prompt. Here are some examples:*

》 I would love to travel to Europe, but I recognize that
I'm too scared to make the trip. I wonder what I can
do about my fear of the unknown.

》 I would love to go dancing, but I know that I hate the
idea of looking ridiculous. How can I get over my
worry about looking foolish?

》 I would love to own a horse, but I don't feel like I'm
entitled to such a luxury. How can I get some inner
permission for such an extravagance?

》 I would love to start a dot.com business, but I don't
feel equal to the task. I wonder how I could gain the
confidence to try?

》 I would love to learn Japanese, but I suspect that I'm
too undisciplined to get very far. Do I have it in me to
become more disciplined?

7. *Add personality change questions to your repertoire of sleep
thinking questions. Try these:*

》 Whenever you're trying to solve a personal problem,
ask yourself the question: What personality change
would help me solve this?

)) One night a week, use a personality change question
as your sleep thinking prompt. For instance, you
could work on a different personality trait every
Wednesday night.

)) Reframe stress reduction issues as personality change
issues by using, for example, the prompt, What in my
own nature is keeping my stress levels up?

)) Remind yourself that, no matter what is bothering
you, your own personality is implicated. Use the
simple prompt How? to stand for the longer question,
How is my personality implicated in my current
problems?

)) Every so often go to bed thinking prompts such as
these: I am really ready for a make-over! or It's time
for a transformation!

8. *Devote a section of your journal to personality change.*
Then try any of the following:

)) On a morning when you don't seem to have anything
to write in your journal, turn to the personality change
section and check in with yourself about your
progress in making your desired personality changes.

)) Make a point of visiting and updating the personality
change section of your journal once a week.

)) Label pages in the personality change section with the
names of the traits you're working on and keep separate track of your progress with each trait.

)) A few times a year, summarize your personality change
work and plan for new changes you'd like to make.

)) On New Year's Eve, before the festivities begin, read
over the personality change section of your journal

and think about what personality work you'd like to accomplish in the coming year.

9. *Pick a behavior you want to change using sleep thinking. Here are some samples:*

    » Use sleep thinking to stop procrastination. Try this as a sleep thinking prompt: Do I procrastinate because I'm anxious?

    » Use sleep thinking to manage a phobia. For instance, you might employ sleep thinking prompts such as these: What would help me become a more comfortable public speaker? or What might help me overcome my fear of flying?

    » Use sleep thinking to reduce your cravings for a food or a drug, using prompts such as these: How can I change my relationship with sugar? How can I end my affair with cocaine?

    » Use sleep thinking to break a compulsion. For instance, if gambling is a problem for you, you might try this prompt: Why am I driven to gamble?

    » Use sleep thinking to overcome shyness. As a sleep thinking prompt, try this: What will help me grow more comfortable in social situations?

10. *Rehearse personality change using sleep thinking. Try one of these:*

    » Before an important conversation, adapt this prompt to your situation: Let me spend tonight practicing what I'm going to say to Bob. Only let me be clearer and more forthright than I usually am.

》 Go to bed with the idea that a coming event is going to turn out well. Use this prompt: Is there anything I need to change in me to assure a good outcome?

》 Invite yourself to rehearse your next big presentation at work during the night, but include this prompt: I want to deliver it with a lot of personal presence. What would that take?

》 If you're anticipating a confrontation, say with your child over his or her grades, wonder the following aloud as you crawl into bed: Let me play out what's going to happen. Can I bring my best self to the moment?

》 Whenever an event that provokes anxiety is looming on the horizon, such as an important meeting, go to bed with a prompt such as this: What strengths of character can I bring to the meeting tomorrow?

11. *Envision personality change using sleep thinking.*
    Here are some samples:

》 Go to bed imagining yourself confidently working on that project that right now seems too difficult to handle.

》 Picture yourself fearlessly embarked on a new course of action and say to yourself, "Let me see how this turns out."

》 Use as a sleep thinking prompt: What would it look like if I accomplished all the changes I dream of making?

》 As another sleep thinking prompt try: Tonight I want a visit from the new me. Or try this one: Tonight I want an excellent dream about my future self.

12. *Reframe problems as possibilities for personality growth. Here are some samples:*

)》 That I haven't been able to write my novel maybe means that I have a perfect opportunity to work on becoming disciplined. Let me look at that tonight.

)》 That I'm tired so much of the time could be a chance for me to investigate whether I take things too seriously. Let me give that some thought.

)》 That Al's problems weigh on me so heavily might be a reminder that I need a life of my own. What about that?

)》 Could my chronic depression be the way I'm letting myself know that I need to change? Is that possible?

)》 Would the troubles I'm having at work be solved if I were a different person at the office? Who would that new me be?

Q. *What if I can't get answers to my sleep thinking questions?*

The first thing to remember is that the results of sleep thinking are often subtle. You may be getting answers and not even knowing it.

You may sleep think a question in April and one day in May, while you're doing the dishes, have an insight about the problem that's been bothering you. You may not connect that insight to your sleep thinking efforts, but, in fact, the answer may be connected and might never have arrived had you not been sleep thinking. In other words, you may get profound results from sleep thinking that you aren't aware are associated with the work you're doing.

However, you may not be on the right track with your question or your line of inquiry. There are many examples throughout this book of sleep thinkers who had to change their sleep thinking question either because it wasn't getting them results or because they sensed that there were better questions to ask themselves. So, it's certainly important that you keep an eye on your sleep thinking question and retain or reject it based on your best understanding of the situation.

Whose Problem Is It?

Many of us know that we have personality issues that we need to address. But this wasn't true for Irene, a psychotherapist in training who came to see me. From Irene's point of view, *other* people had the problem. She came to see me because she was getting negative evaluations at the treatment center where she interned and because professors in her graduate program told her that she had "authority issues." In fact, her supervisor at the treatment center ordered her to do some work on herself, reducing the sting a little by reframing it as "a chance to improve your relationships skills."

Irene explained in great detail all the problems she was having. One professor was lazy and never came prepared to teach, which was why she was always rude to him. She just didn't feel that he deserved respect. Another professor was harsh and punitive and graded unfairly, which was why

Irene was always fighting with her about her grades. A third professor, her internship liaison, seemed nice enough on the surface but was really passive aggressive, saying pleasant things to her face but giving her negative evaluations on her process notes and her case management papers. What was she supposed to do with such a passive-aggressive jerk? At the treatment center, too, a million things were being handled poorly or unfairly. As for her supervisor there, she wanted things done one way, and Irene had very different ideas in mind. So, of course there were going to be conflicts.

I agreed with Irene throughout most of the session. Then I asked her if she could repeat back to me some of the suggestions I had made during the session about how she might handle all these problem people. She couldn't. I asked her why that was. She waved the question away. But I persisted. I reminded her that there was a difference between agreeing with others, which, of course, she didn't have to do, and listening to them, which was actually a part of her job description as a therapist. How could she be a decent therapist if she refused to listen? This comment made her angry, as I knew it would, and she blurted out, "I don't think people have much to say!"

I nodded and continued, "You mean your future clients, too? How will that work?" We sat in silence for some time and finally she said, "I suppose I need to think about that." I described sleep thinking to her and suggested that she spend some time during the week framing sleep thinking questions for herself around the issue of "listening." At the next session she explained, "I tried that stuff out. My question was, Why won't I listen to people? Before I went to bed, I predicted what my answer would be. I thought it would be, I won't listen because people are full of crap. But it was pretty interesting. I got an answer that I wasn't expecting. It was, I won't listen because I won't be controlled. I knew instantly that had to be about my parents. They controlled everything—or rather, they tried to control everything. I hated listening to them because everything they said was manipulative. So that's where it stands."

I agreed with her that what she'd discovered had to be a big part of it. But I wondered whether there weren't other reasons that contributed to her unwillingness to listen. Was it also that she felt superior to most people? She waved that possibility away. But I continued by bringing up the concept of narcissism. I reminded her that as a conceptual matter both healthy narcissism and unhealthy narcissism existed. But what exactly was the difference between the two? I said, "I'm a narcissist. I take it for granted that I know more than you do. I take it for granted that my way is better than your way. I take it for granted that what I want I ought to get. The biographies and autobiographies of well-known people suggest that they, too, were narcissists. But how and where do we draw the line between what's healthy and what's not?"

The next session she came in and said, "I went to bed thinking about what you'd said about narcissism. In the middle of the night, I woke up needing to remind myself just what the diagnostic criteria for a narcissistic personality disorder were. That was an eye-opener. What *healthy* person isn't inclined to react internally to criticism with rage, shame, or humiliation? What *healthy* person doesn't expect to be noticed as special, even without any really special achievements to her credit, simply because she feels special? What *healthy* person doesn't believe that her problems are unique and can be understood only by people who are also special? What *healthy* person isn't often preoccupied with fantasies of unlimited success, brilliance, or ideal love? It was absolutely clear to me what you were saying. If there was no difference on paper between the feelings and desires of a healthy person as opposed to those of a person with a full-blown personality disorder, that had really staggering implications."

I agreed. "So, what can you do to make sure that you stay on the healthy side of narcissism?" She smiled and said that she'd awakened one morning with a phrase running through her head: Put your arrogance in a drawstring bag. Sitting with her journal that morning, she'd written, "I admit that I think that I'm better than other people. But that thought isn't the problem. The problem is operating from that thought in an unaware way. When I'm unaware that my narcissism is showing through, then I come off as grandiose and start to behave in a selfish way. My job is to think highly of myself but to remember that while I *feel* as though I'm the center of the universe, I'd better not *act* that way!" We both laughed. After a few more sessions, we agreed that she should continue sleep thinking but that therapy could come to an end.

$Q.$ *Is sleep thinking an alternative to counseling and psychotherapy?*

If the problem you're experiencing can be resolved by identifying it, learning new things about it, and making some necessary changes, then sleep thinking can do the trick. Counseling and psychotherapy are not medical interventions. They are "thinking" interventions in which one person provides another person with ideas and support. There are many times when you may want the support of another person, so in that sense, any problem may be an appropriate one to take to a therapist. You may also want or need a therapist's ideas, in case the relevant ideas haven't yet occurred to you. I can often help a writer get a sense of what the problem is with her book in a single session, whereas the writer may not get to that realization for months. So there are plenty of good reasons to work with consultants of all sorts. But sleep thinking is a powerful self-help tool that shouldn't be underestimated.

Sleep Thinking as Self-Therapy

Psychodynamic theorists believe that personality calcification begins early on in life and that by the time we're adolescents, we're firmly stuck in the grooves of our formed personality. According to this view, it is miraculous if a person retains any personality flexibility at all. So important is this flexibility that when a psychotherapist spots a little of it in his client, he breathes an involuntary sigh of relief and whispers, "Thank God, I may have a chance here!" If he doesn't encounter it, if he finds himself up against a rigid defensive system, he understands that very little change is likely to happen.

Psychodynamic theorists posit a second essential tyranny as well, the tyranny of the instincts. It is the part of the person that would destroy the world over some small offense or drop his mate at the scent of another creature. Even the so-called mentally healthy person has lusts, rages, and other primitive urges lurking under his rational facade. This darkness is definitely there, all trappings of civilization notwithstanding. In fact, civilization may exist not as an expression of what is highest in us but because without it our low side would cause us to destroy one another.

There is plenty of truth to these two views, that personality is a rigid thing, and that we are more primitive than we imagine. So what are we to do? Dynamic theorists argue for a common-sensical, two-pronged approach: Clients gain awareness and they work on changing. Clients are helped to grow aware of the way their personality is implicated in everything they do, from the way they butter their bread to the way they sabotage themselves at work. Then they are invited to imagine what would constitute useful change. The treatment goals of every psychodynamic school are to bring into awareness important matters that clients currently don't recognize and to aim them in the direction of necessary work.

Given the many reasons each of us has to avoid learning the truth about the way we operate, how are therapists to achieve their goals? Psychoanalysis provides therapists with techniques such as dream work and free association. Transactional analysts invite clients to work with the ego states of adult, parent, and child. Jungians make use of myths, stories, archetypes, and character types. But what actually happens in session, irrespective of the therapist's theoretical position, is virtually identical in all cases. The therapist listens attentively, and when he hears something that sounds important, he says, "Do you want to look at that?" His client either replies, "No!" or "I suppose I'd better."

The therapist's main tasks are selecting the terrain to examine and asking careful, nonthreatening questions. Therapists, therefore, say such things as, "I didn't quite understand that. Do you mean that you didn't tell your boss off because you believed that you were in the wrong or because you were scared that he might fire you? Help me understand what was going on." The therapist may think that he already knows the answer, or he may be asking a genuine question, but what's most important is that he has selected a relevant stopping place and asked his question in a way that doesn't frighten or insult his client.

At such moments, if the stopping has occurred at the right place, the client will say, "That's a good question." In the silence that follows, as she encounters the question and, perhaps for the first time, thinks about it and feels it in the pit of her stomach, awareness is born. This is a profound moment in a person's life. The awareness that arises must still butt heads with the client's calcified personality, which is why insight is not enough. Work must piggyback on the insight if the awareness is to be turned into lasting gain. But the insight is a vital starting point.

All of this should remind you of the sleep thinking you've been doing. You, too, have been inviting self-awareness, mapping out work, and effecting change. Because personality change is hard to accomplish, we need to make a systematic effort in order to produce the change we desire. The sleep thinking program provides that coherence and regularity. You ask yourself important questions in such a way that you don't feel the need to defend yourself against your own answers. You sleep on those questions and eventually answers come. Then, as you process your thoughts each morning, you decide what changes to make and figure out what work will produce those changes. You do the work you've mapped out for yourself, monitor your progress, and continue using sleep thinking to reach your goals. This self-therapy mirrors the best psychotherapy, and the end result is lasting personality change. ((·))

Increasing Your Creativity

My interest in sleep thinking derives from my 30 years as a writer and creativity consultant. I've long known how much work goes on at night as creative people sleep—how symphonies come to composers, novels to writers, paintings to artists, business ideas to entrepreneurs, or scientific ideas to scientists.

Creative Thinking

Composer Ellen Taaffe Zwilich talked about her ability to think creatively both while awake and while asleep:

Somebody I hadn't seen in quite a while called me and asked me if I would be interested in doing a work for their first concert. I said that I didn't have the time, but we kept talking for a while, and during the conversation I started to hear music. The trio was already beginning to take shape in my head. So I said I'd think it over, and I did throughout

> *the rest of the day—and, I guess, through the night as well. In any event, I woke up the next morning and the whole opening section was waiting to be written down.*

Creativity is the word we use for the idea of effectively using our inner resources—our critical thinking skills, our passion, our imagination, our experiences, our knowledge, and so on—on given projects. I've written about why it's so hard for us to make use of these inner resources many times before, in books such as *Fearless Creating* and *The Creativity Book*. Here I want to identify four obstacles to creating and point out how you can use sleep thinking to overcome them.

We have trouble creating for these four reasons:

1. Our personality gets in the way, by issuing us injunctions against making mistakes, berating us about our lack of talent, and so on.

2. Once we get an initial creative idea, there is still lots of hard work to be done in order to turn that idea into a well-crafted, fully realized finished product. That hard work daunts us.

3. Many creative projects do not turn out successfully. Our intuition about the solution to a certain problem turns out to be incorrect, our novel never manages to come to life, and so on. These "failures" are dispiriting and make us less likely to try again.

4. Our creative work has to make its way in the world or else it is just a manuscript in our drawer, a theory on our hard drive, or a canvas stored away in our studio. But the world may not be very interested in what we do, which is another dispiriting obstacle that makes us less likely to try again.

Sleep thinking can help in each of these four areas. It helps us make the kinds of personality changes that transform us into an everyday creative person, someone who creates as a matter of course, tolerates mistakes, trusts that she is talented, and so on. It helps us do the actual work of creating, connecting idea with idea until a whole book is written or a wonder about our family is translated into a personal documentary film. It helps us know whether the work we're doing is on track or whether it ought to be changed or abandoned, and it supplies us with new ideas and new directions to take after we've completed our current project. Last, as was the case with the painter (described earlier) who hated gallery openings, it helps with the marketplace and career issues of the creative person.

All people are inherently creative. But the vast majority of people have pushed the idea of themselves as creative so far down that they never think about it and don't really believe it. Of that vast majority, however, there remains a very large group of people—millions upon millions—for whom the idea of being creative resurfaces regularly. They know that they do not feel good about not using their inner resources, and they wish they could overcome whatever it is that's stopping them from being creative.

They would like to begin to write, paint, compose, invent, or in some other way create. They may already use their natural talents in the service of other people's work, producing great web content at their Internet company or dreaming up terrific ways to manage records at the dental office where they work. But these successes, as good as they can feel, are not a substitute for doing their own creative work. They are missing out on something, and they know it. When you add all of these people to the number of people who are actively creating, you have a very large number. They can all be helped to increase their personal creativity through sleep thinking.

Midwifery and Self-Actualization

Take Louise. A woman in her late 40s, Louise had carved out a life for herself as a midwife to women writers. She helped women write. She lead groups, workshops, and retreats for women, helped them open up and tell their stories for the first time, and for the last five years had even been able to earn a living from this work, albeit a meager one.

But while she knew that she was performing a valuable service, a serious inner conflict remained. She wasn't doing any of her own writing. She couldn't help but agree with her parents and her siblings, who, successful in their professions, wondered why Louise had accomplished so little, given her talents and excellent education. Wasn't Louise supposed to lead as well as serve and create as well as midwife the creations of others? She couldn't quite say whether these were her own ideas, her family's ideas, or ideas embedded in the culture, but she knew for certain that she was carrying around a deep sense of failure.

She helped women heal and grow, but she herself felt wounded and stunted. She started her sleep thinking program with the question, Am I really a writer? This was a painful question to address, because it seemed like there could be no good answer. If she wasn't a writer, that would feel terrible, but if she was a writer, that would only underscore the fact that she'd failed herself. She didn't know what she could gain by sleep thinking this question and began the program a little mournfully, as many sleep thinkers do.

For several nights, she had many dreams, most of them involving a forest at night. She seemed to have been dropped into some fairy tale setting out of the Brothers Grimm, complete with lost children in woolen leggings, wood nymphs, princes disguised as wolves, and princesses disguised as swans. The scenes were mysterious and sometimes frightening, but they didn't seem to have anything to say to her. It was not very different from spending the night at a ballet performance of *Swan Lake.*

She tried a new sleep thinking question: If I were to write, what would I write? The same dreams returned. But now the forest creatures kept changing their gender as well as their identities. Sometimes the wolves were princes; sometimes they were princesses. The same with the swans. Then one night, her dream focused on one wolf, who kept transforming himself before her eyes, morphing from prince to princess and back again over and over. When she woke up, she knew something.

She saw that she was caught in a gender trap and that she had two tasks to perform to get out of it. She had to affirm her work as midwife, to make sure that she did not disparage that part of her nature, but she also had to let her own stories out, to honor that part of her. She'd always known this, but before she'd held it as an either/or proposition. For some reason, it had seemed that she must either serve or lead, that she couldn't do both. Now she wondered why on earth she'd ever thought that. It was as if a model had superimposed itself on her life, the model that one had to be a nurse *or* a doctor, a helper *or* a visionary. Now she saw that she had to be herself.

Instantly, she knew what she wanted to write about: her experiences in India leading writing workshops for untouchable women. She'd gone to India five times and had spent almost a year there altogether. For the longest time, she'd known that she should tell the story of her experiences there, what her Indian students had taught her and what she had taught them, that story intermingled with the sight, smells, and colors of India. It would make for a fascinating and revealing book, if only she could write it. Was she ready? Was it too late for her to begin her life as a writer? She shrugged those questions off and gave herself a new sleep thinking prompt: How shall I start my Indian story?

Time for Seville

In order to unleash one's creativity a person has to make time and space for it. This means more than finding a free hour in the evening and a quiet place in the house in which to work. It means reordering your inner belief system so that creativity rises to the top. It means making time for something that you're not sure you want to do or are capable of doing. Too often, a person decides to wait for "inspiration," which often means that you wait your entire life.

Take Joyce. Joyce was a successful magazine editor who, when she came to see me, had just celebrated her 60th birthday. Over the years, her creativity had manifested itself in overseeing the magazine, picking and editing articles, choosing the covers, and doing the other things that came with her job. As if editing the magazine weren't time-consuming enough, she kept to a strict exercise regimen, did early morning yoga, and served on the board of an organization that raised money for dancers with AIDS. She also gave parties, traveled with her husband, planned vacations with her grown children, and mentored young editors at work, some of whom had gone on to successful careers at other magazines.

Yet all of this was not enough. For the longest time she'd wanted to write a historical novel set in medieval Seville. The setting was clear to her, and she thought that she had the plot and some characters in mind. But she'd never started on the novel, not even to jot down a few notes. A wall stood between her and beginning her book. Each time she thought about the novel, she reminded herself that she was very busy and that each of the things she was doing was valuable in its own right. While that was undeniably true, she still felt that she was failing herself. For more than 40 years, she'd wanted to do some writing, and the fact that she'd never given it a chance disappointed her.

It was clear that Joyce needed to reprioritize her life if she was going to write. We discussed reducing her commitments and even dropping a few of them. I also suggested that she start each day writing her novel rather than in her usual way with yoga, exercise, and journaling. She agreed in a lukewarm way to my suggestions and also agreed to take the following question to bed to sleep think: Where does my writing fit in?

The thought that came to her that very first night was, First thing. She took that to mean that she should start each day writing her novel. But she couldn't pull it off. The next morning she balked and exercised instead. The morning after that she had pressing reasons to get to the office early. The morning after that she again dismissed the idea that she could get up and start writing. Every morning she woke up thinking about writing, but she never got started. By the end of the week, she found herself in a foul mood.

At the next session, I wondered what other sleep thinking question she might try. She didn't seem inclined to continue sleep thinking or motivated to discover what might be preventing her from writing, but in the end, she agreed to try another week of sleep thinking, this time with the prompt, medieval Seville. I wanted her to think about *her book*, not about writing, to see whether that strategy might open the door to her creativity and help her "find time" for her writing. It seemed to me that "medieval Seville" might be a potential opener.

She didn't try sleep thinking either the first or the second night after the session. But the third night she did. Nothing came to her, neither dreams nor thoughts, but she had the sense that some subtle shift had occurred. That day she stole a few minutes during the afternoon between meetings to jot down some notes about Seville as she envisioned it. She saw the narrow back streets in her mind's eye, as she often had, but today she had the insight that a single snarling dog could completely block traffic on such a street. That somehow put her in mind of famous Spanish bull runs, which in turn put her in mind of a runaway bull in the back streets of Seville and what havoc that would wreak.

These were the first actual bits of writing she'd ever done on the book. The next morning, without thinking about it at all, she woke up and went right to the computer. She started a file she labeled "Seville" and began describing the bull, the moonless night, and her heroine. She wrote for more than an hour and then had to rush to make it to work for a meeting. But even as she rushed, she found that she was still thinking about her embryonic novel. She understood that this morning marked the start of her creative life.

Great and Good Work

When Alan and his wife were in their 30s, they purchased a home with a view of the mountains. Alan's wife taught, Alan painted, and together they fashioned a good life, negotiating with unusual success the many hurdles that couples face, including those additional hurdles that arise when one partner is a stay-at-home artist. They raised two children, Alan's wife continued her growth and development as a teacher, and Alan stumbled upon a style of painting—surrealist collage—that began to interest buyers. But despite his success, Alan had the nagging feeling that he was more an entertainer than a real painter. Somehow his core values were not reflected in his collages or in the role he'd stumbled onto as a modern surrealist. While his work was clever, he didn't actually admire its cleverness.

Unlike Louise and Joyce, Alan had spent decades at his creative work. But like many of the creative people I see, he still hadn't found his creative voice. We began to work together on the issue of voice, and I asked him to generate a list of sleep thinking questions that would help him investigate this problem. He came in the next session with a long list that ran the gamut from What is art? to What am I afraid of? I asked him which question on the list seemed most resonant and he selected one from the middle of the list: What if I had to paint as if my life depended on it?

He used that question as a sleep thinking prompt and spent a few dizzying weeks bombarded by dreams that seemed to recapitulate the history of art. In one dream, he was harvesting marble from an Italian quarry. In another, he was living in a narrow Dutch house next to a canal and painting like an old master. In another, he was van Gogh's life drawing teacher, screaming at van Gogh for using greens and purples to make flesh tones. The dreams were very powerful and also very entertaining, even the ones that were like nightmares, but they meant nothing to him.

Then he had a dream that felt different. He was Cézanne or someone like Cézanne, and he had set up his easel in a dark wood. He was painting a landscape incredibly slowly, each brushstroke following the next only after a period of 15 or 20 minutes of observation. Somehow it felt as if he were being punished, and his punishment was to observe objects so carefully and intensely that his eyes burned. But as the dream progressed, he could feel his attitude change. At first it had felt as if something outside of himself was making him paint in this slow, painstaking way. But then he began to accept this way of painting as his own choice. His eyes still burned, but now it was his own idea to stare and examine objects in the landscape before him.

Then someone appeared by his side, in the clearing where he had set up his easel. This bourgeois gentleman made some clucking noises and said, "That is a very muddy painting. No light at all. You should study with someone." He heard himself reply with really startling vehemence, "That's exactly what you said to Cézanne! And you were wrong then, too! Get out of the forest!"

He thought about that dream. But he didn't really know what to make of it. Then, about three weeks later, he glanced out his window at the mountain looming majestic in the distance. He realized that even though he'd been painting for decades, he'd never really inquired about beauty or opened his heart to nature. For the first time, it made profound sense to him why Cézanne had painted and repainted the same mountain landscape for years on end and why other painters, like the Canadian Emily Carr in the Rockies of British Columbia, had done the same thing.

He also realized why he and his wife had bought just this house. It stood in relation to the nearby mountain almost exactly the way Cézanne's house had stood in relation to *his* mountain. Alan sensed that if he were to study this mountain thoroughly, at different times of the day, in different weather conditions, and in different seasons, and paint what he saw and felt, he would get to do something that would allow him to make tangible some feelings he had about love and life that were welling up in him.

Q. *Is there a relationship between sleep thinking and spirituality? I feel things coming up for me as I try to sleep think that I can only call spiritual or soulful.*

There are several reasons why sleep thinking can feel like soulful work. First, any time we make real use of our capabilities, we feel whole and complete, and the name we give to those feelings is "soul" or "spirit." Second, the brain at night does more unusual things than does the brain during the day. It provides us with brilliantly edited stories in our dreams, electrifying nightmares, and so on, and that richness and variety can feel soulful. Third, we have the feeling that we are being helped by a muse or some other creative spirit. This experience can suggest that there's something beyond the individual and that ideas are being transported telepathically around the universe.

I don't know whether these feelings are indeed the presence of soul or whether they simply arise whenever the brain works well and delivers up resonant ideas. I lean toward the secular explanation. But whatever the case, sleep thinkers have these spiritual experiences, just as creators do.

Creativity's Many Faces

Emily, a second generation Chinese-American, had gotten her undergraduate degree in economics and an MBA after that. For 25 years, she'd worked in corporate America in increasingly demanding jobs; during this time she had married and brought two children into the world. But when her 70-year-old aunt was diagnosed with colon cancer and her mother was diagnosed with the same cancer shortly thereafter, something in Emily snapped. It no longer made sense to push herself, her husband, and her children as if nothing but achievement mattered.

But she didn't know what else she should do. She began sleep thinking on the question, What would a more meaningful life look like? One morning she awoke and knew that she had to make a documentary film about the women of her mother's generation, the Chinese women in their 70s and 80s who had grown up in China and about whom she knew almost nothing. In her heart, she knew that her own pursuit of the American Dream had something to do with her feelings about these women, what they stood for and what they demanded of their children, and that she had to come to terms with her feelings while these women were still alive. To honor her realization, Emily began a journey into filmmaking, oral history, and the hidden recesses of her own psyche, which culminated in a film that she never knew she had in her to create.

> If your family is on your mind, you might try this sleep thinking prompt: What can I create with my family as the subject matter?

Joseph, an African-American who went to Yale in the 1960s, had lived through those turbulent times with one foot in the world of the anti-war and Black liberation movements and one foot in the world of personal achievement and mainstream success. He'd landed with both feet in middle America and achieved enough success as a civil engineer to put his children through college and to be able, at 55, to contemplate a comfortable retirement within the next six years. It would be possible to retire to a house by the beach and live there with his wife, the two of them reading, gardening, golfing, playing tennis, taking in jazz concerts, and traveling in the tropics.

He couldn't fault himself for that dream, as his whole adult life had aimed him at exactly that sort of upper-middle-class retirement. But he also knew that something was wrong with that picture. For a while, he thought that what was missing from the vision was some traditional creative outlet and that if he included a little painting or writing in his vision of retirement, it would sit better with him. But when he did some sleep thinking on the matter, he saw that traditional creativity wasn't the answer. He began to realize that his deepest principles demanded that he lend a helping hand to others. But what was that to be? Had he community activism in mind, perhaps involving low-cost housing issues or AIDS awareness? He didn't know, but he continued sleep thinking the matter.

Then he had a dream whose message seemed absolutely clear to him. He wanted to help African-American children. With his wife's blessing, he began to investigate the world of foster parenting. To his surprise, he discovered that being with young children activated his creative nature in a way that private creativity never had. Drawing with a boy of six or telling stories to a girl of nine felt better than sitting in front of a canvas or a computer screen, and the rewards felt truly spectacular. He loved the smiles and laughter of young children, and he loved that he was helping them think, create, and grow. He knew that his retirement had to include this sort of creativity.

Do you identify in a deep way with some group? What would you like to create that serves or is informed by that group identification?

Loretta was a young woman who hated making mistakes. She had grown up with critical parents who made her feel worthless whenever she displeased them, which, since nothing could ever be done to their liking, was all the time. If she played a piano piece pretty well at recital, they could only comment on the way she'd slouched, on how shy she'd seemed, or on how much better they'd expected her to play, considering all the lessons she'd taken. If she ate all the food on her plate, they wondered if she was trying to fatten herself up, and if she left food, they wondered whether she knew how much a year's worth of groceries cost. Loretta could do nothing right.

The result of their meanness was to ruin her ability to freely make mistakes. She still made mistakes, since we all do, but she hated them and tried to hide them from herself and from everyone else. But she couldn't really hide them and ended up chastising herself, saying, "Only a champion idiot like me could make these many mistakes." Finally, she realized that she had to change her attitude, since her fear of mistakes was ruining her ability to write papers in her graduate psychology program. Because she felt that each paper had to be perfect, she couldn't start them; then, at the last minute, she'd grind something out. What she turned out was never as good as the paper she might have written if she'd felt free to write multiple drafts.

Desperate, she began to sleep think, choosing this statement, instead of a question, as her prompt: I am so scared of mistakes. On about the third or fourth night, she had a dream about mud. It wasn't just any mud; it was the kind of mud you make when you mix too many pigments together. It was painter's mud. What she saw in the dream was a happy child obliviously mixing many colors together, making a face at the mud she produced, and blithely starting over. The child in the dream just didn't care that she had wasted some paint. It simply wasn't a tragedy or an issue at all. No word like *mistake, failure, stupid, wasteful,* or *incompetent* even crossed the little girl's mind. Loretta made the pledge to herself that somehow she would learn to become like that little girl. She choose as her mantra, Mud means nothing.

Do you have the hunch that something in your past or in your personality is preventing you from creating? If you do, that's worth a full-scale sleep thinking investigation.

Howard's roadblock was envy. As a teenager, Howard had lived for his guitar. Throughout high school and college, he played in bands, and several times a week his band would perform at parties or in local clubs. A couple of the bands built up a regular following, and one of the bands got so well known that someone from a record label came out to see them play. But nothing came of that, and after college, Howard chose to work in a friend's business rather than live the marginal life of a rock musician. For a while, he kept up his guitar playing, but after a few years, he had to stop.

A couple of his friends from college went on to make it in famous bands, which made Howard feel even worse about his decision to choose the safer life course. Intellectually, he knew what a toll the rock life and the rock business took on people and how long the odds were against him becoming a star. But viscerally he felt cheated, disappointed, and envious of all successful musicians. That envy prevented him from playing the guitar for fun and even from enjoying music, which had always been the love of his life.

Over the years, he built up a successful kitchen and bathroom remodeling business, but in his own mind, he felt like a loser. It still haunted him that he'd never become famous, and it still made him furious that he had to work in the ordinary world, even though that world was paying him well, while a fortunate few got to make music for a living. At the same time he missed making music. He wished that he could enter into some new relationship with music that would allow him to enjoy it without all those painful feelings of envy welling up and consuming him.

He bought a synthesizer, to see whether making music that way would satisfy him. But it didn't. He tried learning the Japanese flute, whose sound intrigued him, but after a while, he gave that up. Each attempt to find a new way to make music led nowhere. When he came to see me, shortly after his 51st birthday, I asked him whether he should work on the envy directly and deal with that pain. Reluctantly, Howard agreed that he should. He chose this sleep thinking question: How can I live with the knowledge that others made it at music and I didn't?

For weeks, nothing came to him. He went about his business, more irritably than usual, but made himself continue sleep thinking.

Each night he posed himself a question, and each morning he wrote in his journal. He recorded many strange dreams that he was sure held no special meaning and many idea fragments that he couldn't piece together. But after about two months, he woke up with the strangest feeling. Nothing that he could name had come to him—not a dream, not an idea, not an intuition, nothing—and yet he felt transformed. What he heard himself say was, "I can play music." That very day he went to a guitar store. The long sleep thinking process had helped him resolve issues and come to a new understanding of his situation, without an "answer" ever presenting itself.

Should you return to some creative outlet that you abandoned, for whatever reasons, a long time ago?

Janet had raised two children with her husband Mark. She and Mark had a decent if distant relationship, and their children appeared to be quite successful, getting good grades in school and participating in all sorts of extracurricular activities. Their daughter Elizabeth was an excellent tennis player and their son Alex was his soccer team's star forward. From the outside, everything about Janet's family life looked ideal.

But Janet, who worked outside the house at a large company and who chalked up her inability to write to the fact that she had no time for it, was still suffering in her early 40s from a trauma that dated back to her late teens.

Before Mark, there had been another man in Janet's life. During that relationship, Janet had become pregnant, had their baby, and given it up for adoption. Ever since, the abiding messages in Janet's brain were "I'm evil" and "I don't deserve anything good happening." This self-hatred led directly to self-censorship and prevented Janet from writing, or so I surmised. Janet angrily disagreed with my hunch. She retorted that giving up her child had nothing to do with her writing block and that dwelling on that event couldn't possibly help. In fact, she really didn't think that we could work together, so offbase was my hunch. She left and didn't come back.

Two years later, I ran into Janet at a writers' conference. She came up to tell me that she was looking for her son and writing about the search. After stopping therapy, she'd had a dream about a session, in which she was the client and her grown-up son was the therapist. What was most important about the dream experience was that her son didn't seem to hate her. She couldn't really hear what they were saying, but she could tell by the way he sometimes smiled and by his general demeanor that though he was asking her tough questions, he wasn't being critical of her. By the end of the dream, she knew that she wanted to find him.

Standing there in the hotel lobby, she grudgingly admitted that burying the experience of giving up her child for adoption had probably tied her in knots and prevented her from writing. But she was nevertheless still angry with me for having been the messenger who'd delivered that news. Couldn't I have waited longer or been more subtle in delivering it? When she finished, I nodded and wished her well, entirely satisfied that our brief time together had provoked the sleep thinking she had desperately needed to do.

> Is there a big secret, something that you're ashamed of or that's badly upsetting you, that's also preventing you from creating? If so, try this sleep thinking prompt: How can I get free?

Marsha, a retired anthropology professor, and her husband Charles, a retired history professor, had lived a good life. They had shared in the raising of three children, minded each other's need for solitude, and supported each other's personal and professional growth. Well known in their professions, they had every intention of continuing to write and contribute until feebleness overtook them. But their first couple of years of retirement seemed to zip by without either of them getting much work done. There always seemed to be letters and e-mail to answer, trips to the children and grandchildren to make, and naps to be taken. Life was good, but Marsha felt that she was accomplishing too little as precious time slipped away.

She began sleep thinking on the generic question, What am I supposed to do? The answer came to her in a dream. She saw a second house, by the ocean, to which sometimes she and sometimes Charles retreated. When she awoke and analyzed the dream, the idea seemed silly, since they had a quiet, beautiful house already and no apparent need for another one. But the more Marsha thought about it—and the longer she went without working on her current book—the more she realized that a retreat home was a necessity and not a luxury. Together, she and Charles found a tiny place by the sea, four hours' drive from their home. On her first retreat there, Marsha got more writing done in a week than she'd gotten done in the previous two years.

> Is there one thing you need to do in order to get sarted on your creative life? Is that a good question to sleep think?

You, too, can use sleep thinking to help you launch and complete creative projects and live a more creative life. The following are some good sleep thinking prompts. Try one out tonight.

1. What do I want to create?

2. What obstacles stand between me and creating?

3. Do I have permission from myself to create?

4. Do I view myself as creative?

5. Do I have the patience to work long and hard on a creative project?

6. If my first creative efforts don't please me, will I quit?

7. Must I have reasons to create or can I just "do it"?

8. Does part of me consider creating a waste of time?

9. Will my anxiety get in the way of my creativity?

10. Am I too busy to create?

11. Am I too uncentered to create?

12. What's pressing inside of me that wants to be born?

13. Am I afraid that I have no ideas and nothing to say?

14. Do I believe that I count enough to create?

15. What would be a good first step to unleash my creativity?

You may suppose that solving your problems, reducing your stress, and upgrading your personality are more important things to think about than increasing your creativity. But you might want to reconsider. For one thing, the changing face of work brought about by our latest technological revolution demands that we manifest our creativity. It turns out that every 21st-century worker will have to be creative, ready or not. And if you use sleep thinking to increase your creativity, you'll also improve your job performance and aid your career. When all is said and done, creativity is just another name for making use of our talents and capabilities, and each of us longs to do just that. ((·))

Postscript: Working the Sleep Thinking Program

You already sleep think, since everyone is a sleep thinker. But you may not be formally working the sleep thinking program yet. If you aren't, that's understandable. Maybe you didn't see its value, or maybe you didn't feel motivated to do the required work. Or maybe spending an hour first thing each morning with a journal seemed just too hard. But I wonder if you might be willing to give the program a try now, even for just one week.

If you work a 9 to 5 job and are off on the weekends, wait until Friday to get started. Take some time on Friday evening going over the steps of the program, creating your sleep thinking list of questions, and choosing an initial question. Go to bed Friday night with a sleep thinking question in mind. Whatever time you arise on Saturday, spend that first hour thinking about the question you posed yourself and anything else that comes to you as you sit with your journal.

A few times during the day on Saturday, remind yourself that you're trying out the program for a week. Consider what question you'll take to bed with you Saturday night. It might be the one from Friday night, or it might be a new one (because you've learned something already). On Saturday night, go to bed a little earlier than usual. On Sunday morning, whenever you awaken, spend the first hour with your journal.

On Sunday night, your mind will almost certainly turn to the coming week at work. But try to stick with your sleep thinking ritual, even if you feel anxious or distracted. When you wake up Monday morning, it may feel impossible to spend any time with your journal. But see if you can give it at least five or ten minutes.

On Monday night, after a long day at work, you'll be tired, and your mind will be full of work-related matters. Again, try to stay with the program, even if you do nothing more than murmur your sleep thinking question to yourself a few times before falling asleep. For the rest of the week, do whatever feels possible, and don't worry if you miss steps here or there.

On Friday, try to summarize for yourself what the week was like.

I hope you'll e-mail me the summary report of your first week's efforts. I'd love to know how it went, and I'll try to share what I learn in future books. The best way to communicate is via e-mail, which you can send to *amaisel@sirius.com*.

You may also want to visit my Web sites: *www.sleepthinking.com* and *www.ericmaisel.com*. I hope they will become valuable resources for people interested in sleep thinking. I intend to post comments from readers and other relevant information there. You can also reach me at my fax/message machine number: 925-689-0210. Or you can reach me via regular mail, Eric Maisel, Ph.D., P. O. Box 613, Concord, CA 94522-0613.

You don't need any additional training or tools in order to sleep think. However, I offer workshops, and you might enjoy

attending one of them. But just following the program outlined here will net you the results you want.

I'd love to better understand every detail of your sleep
thinking process: which questions seemed to work and which
didn't, how you dealt with partial answers or information you
couldn't decipher, and so on. Anything you share with me will
prove of value to all of us. By sharing, we can begin to spread
the news about this terrific problem-solving tool—our brain at
night—that each of us has at our disposal.

P.S. Don't miss my free monthly newsletters! One will
keep you posted on sleep thinking and the other with your creative life. To subscribe, just visit *www.sleepthinking.com* or
www.ericmaisel.com. ((◦))

Resources

I hope that the various resources listed here prove useful to you.

When new books of interest come to my attention, I'll post them on my Web sites: *www.ericmaisel.com* and *www.sleepthinking.com*. If there are books you like that I've missed, please let me know about them.

Anxiety and Stress Management

Bourne, Edmund. *Anxiety and Phobia Workbook*. New York: New Harbinger Press, 1995.

Davidson, Jeff. *The Complete Idiot's Guide to Managing Stress*. New York: MacMillan, 1996.

Davis, Martha. *The Relaxation and Stress Reduction Workbook*. New York: Fine Communications, 1997.

Dupont, Robert. *The Anxiety Cure*. New York: John Wiley and Sons, 1998.

Gerzon, Robert. *Finding Serenity in an Age of Anxiety*. New York: Bantam Doubleday, 1998.

Goldman, Carol. *Overcoming Panic, Anxiety, and Phobias*. New York: Whole Person Associates, 1996.

Goliszek, Andrew. *60 Second Stress Management*. New York: New Horizon Press, 1992.

Peurifoy, Renean. *Anxiety, Phobias, and Panic*. New York: Warner Books, 1995.

The Brain

Damasio, Antonio. *Descartes' Error*. New York: Putnam, 1994.

Dennett, Daniel. *Consciousness Explained*. Boston: Little, Brown and Company, 1991.

Edelman, Gerald. *Bright Air, Brilliant Fire*. New York: Basic Books, 1992.

Greenfield, Susan. *Journey to the Centers of the Mind*. New York: W. H. Freeman, 1995.

Hobson, J. Allan. *The Chemistry of Conscious States*. Boston: Little, Brown and Company, 1994.

Humphrey, Nicholas. *A History of the Mind*. New York: Simon and Schuster, 1992.

Pinker, Steven. *How the Mind Works*. New York: W. W. Norton, 1997.

Creativity

Boden, Margaret. *The Creative Mind*. New York: HarperCollins, 1992.

Cameron, Julia. *The Artist's Way*. New York: Tarcher/Putnam, 1992.

Edwards, Betty. *Drawing on the Right Side of the Brain*. New York: Tarcher/Putnam, 1999.

Maisel, Eric. *Affirmations for Artists*. New York: Tarcher/ Putnam, 1996.

Maisel, Eric. *The Creativity Book*. New York: Tarcher/Putnam, 2000.

Maisel, Eric. *Deep Writing*. New York: Tarcher/Putnam, 1999.

Maisel, Eric. *Fearless Creating*. New York: Tarcher/Putnam, 1995.

Maisel, Eric. *A Life in the Arts*. New York: Tarcher/Putnam, 1994.

Maisel, Eric. *Living the Writer's Life*. New York: Watson-Guptill, 1999.

Phillips, Jan. *Marry Your Muse*. Wheaton, IL: Quest Books, 1997.

Pierce-Meyers, Tona, ed. *The Soul of Creativity*. Novato, CA: New World Library, 1998.

Warner, Susan. *Making Room for Making Art*. Chicago, IL: Chicago Review Press, 1994.

Dreams and Dreaming

Delaney, Gail. *All about Dreams*. San Francisco, CA: Harper, 1998.

Devereux, Paul. *The Lucid Dreaming Kit*. New York: Journey Editions, 1998.

Epel, Naomi. *Writers Dreaming*. New York: Random House, 1993.

Garfield, Patricia. *Creative Dreaming*. New York: Simon and Schuster, 1995.

Harary, Keith. *Lucid Dreaming in Thirty Days*. New York: St. Martin's Press, 1989.

Hobson, J. Allan. *The Dreaming Brain*. New York: HarperCollins, 1988.

Laberge, Stephen. *Exploring the World of Lucid Dreaming*. New York: Ballantine Books, 1991.

Mazza, Joan. *Dreaming Your Real Self*. New York: Perigee, 1998.

Peters, Roderick. *Living with Dreams*. London: Rider, 1990.

Reed, Henry. *Dream Solutions*. San Rafael, CA: New World Library, 1991.

Taylor, Jeremy. *Dream Work*. Ramsey, NJ: Paulist Press, 1983.

Personality Growth and Change

Heatherton, Todd. *Can Personality Change?* Washington, DC: American Psychological Association, 1997.

Kagan, Jerome. *Gaden's Prophecy: Temperament in Human Nature*. New York: Basic Books, 1997.

Katz, Mark. *On Playing a Poor Hand Well*. New York: W. W. Norton: 1997.

Kegan, Robert. *The Evolving Self*. Cambridge, MA: Harvard University Press, 1983.

Lewis, Michael. *Altering Fate*. New York: Guilford Press, 1998.

Littauer, Florence. *Personality Plus*. New York: Fleming Rewell Co., 1992.

Matthews, Gerald. *Personality Traits*. New York: Cambridge University Press, 1998.

Morris, Lois. *The New Personality Self-Portrait*. New York: Bantam, 1995.

Wright, William. *Born That Way: Genes, Behavior, and Personality*. New York: Routledge, 1999.

Sleep

Alvarez, A. *Night*. New York: W. W. Norton, 1995.

Borbely, Alexander. *Secrets of Sleep*. New York: Basic Books, 1986.

Coren, Stanley. *Sleep Thieves*. New York: The Free Press, 1996.

Hobson, J. Allan. *Sleep*. New York: Scientific American Press, 1995.

Horne, James. *Why We Sleep*. New York, Oxford University Press, 1988.

Kavey, Neil. *50 Ways to Sleep Better*. Lincolnwood, IL: Publications International, 1996.

Kleitman, Nathaniel. *Sleep and Wakefulness*. Chicago: University of Chicago Press, 1963

Lavie, Peretz. *The Enchanted World of Sleep*. New Haven, CT: Yale University Press, 1996.

Moore-Ede, Martin, and Suzanne LeVert. *The Complete Idiot's Guide to Getting a Good Night's Sleep*. New York: Simon and Schuster, 1998.

Index